GRAND SLAM
Champions

GRAND
Cha

SLAM

mpions

The Official Story
of England's
Undefeated Season

BY TEAM ENGLAND RUGBY

ORION

First published in Great Britain in 2003 by Orion
an imprint of Orion Books Ltd
Orion House, 5 Upper St Martin's Lane, London WC2H 9EA

A CIP catalogue record for this book is available from the British Library

ISBN 0 75286 047 X

Designed by Harry Green
Photographs supplied by Getty Images

Printed and bound by Butler & Tanner Ltd,
Frome and London

Contents

Foreword by Clive Woodward 6

Introduction 8

England v New Zealand 10

England v Australia 26

England v South Africa 38

England v France 54

Wales v England 68

England v Italy 80

England v Scotland 94

Ireland v England 108

New Zealand v England 122

Australia v England 140

World Cup details 158

Picture Credits 160

Foreword
by Clive Woodward

I'm delighted to be writing the foreword for the official RFU's *Grand Slam Champions*. The book looks back at the England squad's successful 2002/3 season, notable for victories against all three Southern Hemisphere sides last November, a Grand Slam and a successful summer tour of New Zealand and Australia in June, which included wins against the New Zealand Maoris, the All Blacks and the Wallabies.

Grand Slam Champions vividly captures the events leading up to each of the tests last season in words and pictures along with the key moments from the matches themselves. Ian Stafford has put together an accurate commentary on the games derived from his own observations and comments taken from the players and coaches both before and after the matches.

England were asked a number of questions last season: namely that whether we were unable to win away from home, play on hard and fast surfaces or in difficult conditions. While I believe that we provided the answers, the tight finishes in the home games against New Zealand and Australia in the autumn Investec Challenge Series and the away fixture against the All Blacks in June highlighted how fine the line is between victory and defeat in international rugby.

The win against New Zealand was only the second time an England side had beaten the All Blacks away from home, while the victory against the Wallabies in Melbourne was a first away win in Australia. Going into those games the whole squad was mindful of England's track record in the Southern Hemisphere and the results and memories from those matches will stay with the fans, players and coaches for a long time to come. I'd also like to thank Zurich for their support of the tour.

To win a Grand Slam last season was a highlight for everyone connected with the squad. There was huge speculation that the RBS Six Nations Championship would be decided by the opening fixture between England and France but we all knew that the Championship would be a difficult one with all the sides continuing to progress. The Ireland team we faced in Dublin at the end of March played well throughout the Championship and proved how tough they were when they came back from behind to beat Wales in Cardiff, courtesy of a Ronan O'Gara drop goal in injury time. Therefore, to beat Ireland by a margin of 42–6 was a performance we were all proud of. Italy also continue to progress, beating Wales in Rome and for an hour producing an excellent display at Twickenham. At the Millennium Stadium the Welsh, under the captaincy of Jonathan Humphreys, asked us some serious questions, and Scotland gave a good account of themselves against us and in South Africa during the summer. France proved yet again, in a number of games, that they are always dangerous.

The book captures the highlights of all of England's test matches last season so please enjoy it as we start our preparations for the Rugby World Cup in October.

CLIVE WOODWARD
England Head Coach

Introduction

Ever since rugby turned professional, the England national rugby team has promised so much but has failed, just, and on occasions agonisingly, to deliver. For a team so dominant, so destructive and so talented, there has been little to show for all their efforts, and for the entertainment that they have provided the world of rugby.

This is not to denigrate the England team. They, more than anyone else, understand their failings. They have grown stronger as the years have passed by, and especially since Head Coach Clive Woodward took charge in 1997.

Heavy defeats to the Southern Hemisphere were turned into first narrow losses and then victories against the giants of Australia, New Zealand and South Africa. Meanwhile, against European opposition, England broke the mid-nineties dominance of the French in the Five (later Six) Nations and were pre-eminent in the Triple Crown.

Yet still they lost the games that really mattered. Defeat to New Zealand in a World Cup pool game in 1999 resulted in a schedule that proved too tough, with elimination from the competition coming at the hands of South Africa in the quarter-final. A last-gasp defeat to Wales, also in 1999, cost England a Grand Slam. Another loss, this time in Scotland a year later, left England with the Five Nations Championship, but still no Grand Slam. A third consecutive Slam was lost in 2001 on the final weekend of the championship, this time in Ireland. The next year the agony came early: France deservedly won in Paris and then did not slip up in later matches, gaining a Grand Slam for themselves.

The 2002–3 season therefore promised to be quite a challenge for Clive Woodward's England squad. Three back-to-back test matches in the autumn Investec Challenge Series were scheduled against the big three from the Southern Hemisphere. Then, in the RBS Six Nations, England would be looking for their first Grand Slam in eight years. Finally, a June tour Down Under would pitch the team against New Zealand and Australia in their own back yards.

After all that, there was the small matter of the World Cup in Australia, which added extra significance and pressure to all of the games played up to then.

England finally seemed to have the perfect cocktail for success: talent and experience, inspirational leadership under Martin Johnson, an awesome set of forwards and an adventurous group of backs, and a world-class management team led by Woodward. It looked as if the stage was set for all of the recent wrongs to be put right.

In this account of England's season to the end of June 2003, we shall look back on a stunning autumn, a sensational RBS Six Nations campaign and a ground-breaking antipodean tour. A lot of rugby has been played, a lot of points scored and a lot of lessons learned. For every member of the England squad, these eight months will be a period of their lives they will never forget.

It all started back in November 2002, when the mighty New Zealand All Blacks came to Twickenham.

ENGLAND
31

NEW ZEALAND
28

Saturday, 9 November 2002 at Twickenham

ENGLAND

Robinson, Simpson-Daniel (Healey, 78), Greenwood (Johnston, 40), Tindall, Cohen, Wilkinson, Dawson, Woodman, Thompson, Vickery, Johnson, Grewcock (Kay, 61), Moody, Dallaglio, Hill (Back, 49–62)

Subs (not used): Regan, Leonard, Stimpson

Tries

Moody, Wilkinson, Cohen

Conversions

Wilkinson 2

Penalties

Wilkinson 3

Drop Goal

Wilkinson

NEW ZEALAND

Blair, Howlett, Umaga, Lowen (M. Robinson, 47), Lomu, Spencer (Mehrtens, 40), Devine (Lee, 30), McDonnell, Hore, Meeuws, Williams, K. Robinson (Mika, 62), Randell, Broomhall, Holah

Subs (not used): Mealamu, Hayman, So'oialo

Tries

Lomu 2, Howlett, Lee

Conversions

Blair 2, Mehrtens 2

Referee

Jonathan Kaplan (South Africa)

Attendance

75,000

CHAPTER ONE

'We got what we wanted out of this game and this was a win'

The international season and the start of what would be a mammoth twelve months for England would kick off with just about the most anticipated test match of them all. Those Down Under in Sydney and Johannesburg may quibble with this, as would the 2002 Six Nations and Grand Slam champions France, but, as the forthcoming season would prove, England versus the All Blacks was the best of the Northern Hemisphere against the best of the Southern. Those who witnessed this memorable game inside a packed, 75,000-capacity-filled Twickenham, were not disappointed.

ABOVE Making a splash: England in wet-weather training before the All Blacks match.

Unlike Australia and South Africa, New Zealand were infrequent visitors to these shores. When they had made the journey, it usually ended in misery for the English. Indeed, in twenty-three test matches between the two sides England had won just four, the most recent being a decade ago. That 15–9 victory was best remembered for Jamie Joseph's first-minute stamp on debutante scum-half Kyran Bracken's ankle. Since then, apart from a credible 26–26 draw at Old Trafford in 1997, England had experienced nothing but defeat, beginning with the 1995 World Cup semi-final in Cape Town in which a new kid named Jonah Lomu demolished Will Carling's men with four super-human tries. Defeat at Twickenham followed a fortnight after the 1997 draw. The next year saw two heavy beatings when a severely depleted England squad ventured south to Auckland and Dunedin on what was later dubbed the 'Tour of Hell'. Finally, in October 1999, came yet another loss to the All Blacks, this time in a World Cup group game at Twickenham. In what was a far tighter affair, the key to New Zealand's victory was once again Lomu, who scored the crucial try of the game as only he could.

Although England still qualified for the quarter-final, they lost to the five drop goals of South African Jannie de Beer. It could be said that the defeat to New Zealand more or less cost them any chance of winning the tournament. Instead of qualifying in first place from their group, England were forced to play a physically demanding play-off against the bruising Fijians, and then face the Springboks just four days later in Paris. It was too much.

But that was four years ago. Since then England, under the careful guidance of Head Coach Clive Woodward, his coaches, and the strong leadership of captain Martin Johnson, had turned Twickenham into a fortress. Indeed, that World Cup group game against New Zealand was the last time England had tasted defeat at home. Since then they had strung together a winning run of fifteen games, including four straight wins over world champions Australia and South Africa. The gap was clearly closing between the Northern and Southern Hemisphere teams, led by England's advance.

New Zealand arrived in England as something of an

ABOVE The formidable haka led by Jonah Lomu.

unknown quantity. Long gone were their days of global dominance. For much of the past decade they had suffered at the hands of the Wallabies in the Tri-Nations, Bledisloe and World Cups. Yet the word from Auckland, Wellington, Christchurch and Dunedin was that new, young and fresh faces were ready to take the international game by storm.

Their new coach, John Mitchell, knew a thing or two about Clive Woodward and his England team. Mitchell had served as Woodward's assistant coach, particularly in the role of forwards' coach, as well as first playing and then coaching both Sale and Wasps. His last game with England before returning home to coach Waikato was the rather ignominious loss in the sleet and wind of Murrayfield in 2000 against Scotland, a shock defeat that cost the team the Grand Slam. Since then, however, Mitchell had impressed back home to the extent that when Wayne Smith resigned from his post as New Zealand head coach in the early summer of 2002,

Mitchell fulfilled his long-cherished dream of taking over at the helm of the All Blacks.

Mitchell was determined to experiment with the squad he chose to travel to the Northern Hemisphere on a short tour that would begin in England and also include France and Wales. All eight members of the pack on duty last time out for the Tri-Nations decider in Durban twelve weeks previously were left at home, as were the majority of the backs. Only Tana Umaga, Andrew Mehrtens and Doug Howlett came from that starting fifteen. Howlett had already proved to be one of the finds of the international year.

And then there was Jonah Lomu. His form, undermined by injuries and a chronic kidney disorder, had been so poor that it was unlikely he would have been selected for the tour if Mitchell had not left twenty capped players at home, all reportedly injured.

Mitchell's stance on Lomu was purposefully withering: 'Every player has been selected on merit with the exception of Jonah Lomu,' he announced. 'Frankly, we are sick of waiting for him to show form. He is hanging in there on past form, so this is a really critical time for him. He is going to have to show improvement.'

England, too, faced potential problems in the fortnight before the opening test. The first-choice starting fifteen had not played together since winning in Rome the previous April in the final Six Nations international. Thereafter, many of England's better-known names had been rested over the summer, or had undergone overdue surgery. Under the impressive leadership of stand-in captain Phil Vickery, a weakened England side nevertheless inflicted defeat on Argentina in Buenos Aires, no mean feat for any

international side to achieve. Performances on tour in South America threatened the more established old guard, and gave Clive Woodward the kind of selection dilemma all coaches crave.

Two of England's more settled players, Will Greenwood and Martin Johnson, had been hit by personal traumas. For Greenwood, the lanky Harlequins centre considered one of the most creative backs in the game, the loss of his baby boy Freddie in September hit him understandably hard. Supported by his club, family and friends, and by the world of rugby in general, he was determined to make it to the autumn internationals, and did so on merit alone. Johnson, the twice Lions and Leicester captain, had been

going through a difficult time, too. Losing the captaincy against Wales during the previous Six Nations due to suspension, he was then selected only to sit on the bench for that final international in Rome. With the likes of Ben Kay and Danny Grewcock challenging hard, there were even questions raised in the media over whether Johnson's time had come. And then, far worse than any of this, came the death of his mother from cancer. That put his other problems into perspective, of course, but must have been especially hard to handle at the end of a tough season.

Clive Woodward had no doubts, however. When reappointing Johnson as captain he also named Vickery and Jonny Wilkinson as joint vice-captains, therefore provid-

ing the next extraordinary step in Wilkinson's extraordinary career.

'It's another achievement I'm very happy to notch up,' Wilkinson admitted, on hearing the news. 'It serves as a huge boost to my confidence. It allows me to be more authoritative, and far more accountable for every decision and action I take. It enables me to make an impression, which is precisely what a fly-half should be doing. A quiet and reserved fly-half is normally a bad fly-half. So I'm delighted to become vice-captain, and I hope I continue to be so for the foreseeable future.'

The England Head Coach did not stop there, either, when it came to surprises. In selecting Leicester's Lewis

Moody, Woodward dismantled the longest-serving back row combination in test rugby. Neil Back, who a year before had captained England to three autumn test wins out of three, suddenly found himself on the bench. Richard Hill, who would win his fiftieth cap, was switched to cover Back's position of open-side flanker, with Moody at blind-side and Lawrence Dallaglio at number eight. Dallaglio was making his first appearance in eighteen months for England after shattering his kneecap in a club game. Back, ever the team player, took his surprise omission on the chin. 'It's an indication of the strength of the squad England have now got and not anything to do with my international days being numbered,'

ABOVE Ecstasy and agony: Lewis Moody a split-second
before scoring a try and being squashed by the All Blacks.

he insisted, a prophecy that would shortly be proven correct. 'I am thrilled Lewis is getting a run. My immediate
task is to do whatever I can to ensure we beat New
Zealand, to channel all my energy into ensuring the back
row have the best possible preparation and that my contribution helps guarantee that they gel as a unit.'
Woodward explained, 'I have picked the form back row.
Neil is playing as well as ever but then so is Richard Hill
and I've wanted for some time to get Lewis into the starting fifteen. With Lawrence getting better every game he
plays, we have picked from huge strength.'

Moody knew of his call up to the starting fifteen before
Woodward made the official announcement to the team.
'At lunch Neil came up and congratulated me,' he recalled.
'I assumed Neil was playing as well until he told me that
he was on the bench. It took a lot for him to congratulate
me under the circumstances, and I wasn't quite sure what

to say. The funny thing is I always felt I'd be picked for
England ahead of Neil before it happened at Leicester, our
club. It had taken a long time for me to get the better of
him, but every day running up to the New Zealand game
Neil helped me.'

It was a personal triumph for Moody, especially when
just the year before he had considered leaving Leicester
after the Tigers had signed the All Black legend Josh
Kronfeld. This meant that Moody faced the prospect of
having to oust both Back and Kronfeld in order to play
regular first-team rugby. 'I had lots of offers to move on
and it was a big decision for me to stay at Leicester,'
Moody reflected. 'I didn't want to leave until I had proven
myself. I hadn't achieved my goals there and I felt there was
unfinished business to complete. Funnily enough, Josh's
arrival boosted me. I knew then that I would be competing against Back and Kronfeld, the two best open-side
flankers in the modern game, but vastly different in the
way they play. I knew I could learn from both of them.'

Elsewhere, Matt Dawson came back into the side at
scrum-half and Cornishman Trevor Woodman would

make his first start for England at loose head. Twenty-year-old James Simpson-Daniel was selected to face Jonah Lomu, just six months after having given the big All Black the runaround when playing for an England fifteen against the Barbarians. Conceding seven inches and almost six stones to the Kiwi, it would be a case of little versus large out on the wing, with Simpson-Daniel winning his first cap against the most daunting of opponents. Simpson-Daniel, known as 'Little Sinbad' by his teammates after a nickname that stemmed back to his Sedbergh School days, was under no illusions about the task awaiting him. He knew that six months earlier he had been up against a fun-seeking Barbarians side in an end-of-season friendly. Now he faced a Lomu desperately trying to save his career playing in a depleted but still talented All Blacks side in a test match. 'I managed to get around Lomu once but people seem to forget that he brushed me aside two or three times as well,' Simpson-Daniel reminded people. 'I am shocked and delighted that the management have had the confidence to pick me. I know he's huge, but I'm used to playing against bigger opponents.'

To add to the youngster's tension, Lomu, unusually, would stay silent throughout the week running up to the test. The normally affable and talkative All Black made it known that he would not be speaking at all about the game, preferring to keep his own counsel. 'This is one of the most important test matches of his life and he wants to do all his talking on the field,' announced an All Blacks spokesman. Ominous words for Simpson-Daniel, and for an England team ravaged several times by Lomu over the preceding seven years.

With only Lomu and Howlett selected as wingers in the squad, both were assured of their places in the New Zealand starting fifteen. Like Woodward, however, Mitchell was to spring a few surprises himself when he came to naming his team to face England. The biggest shock concerned two of his most established and renowned players: Andrew Mehrtens could only make the bench, while Christian Cullen was omitted completely from the twenty-two-man squad. Mehrtens, just five points short of becoming only the fourth player in test history to reach 900 points, lost out to stand-off Carlos Spencer, recalled after a two-year absence on the strength of his displays with Auckland's championship-winning team. Cullen, boasting a phenomenal strike rate of 46 tries from just 57 tests, had not shown anything like that form in recent

BELOW A virtuoso try from Jonny Wilkinson.

months. He had already lost his place during the Tri-Nations to Leon MacDonald. Now, with MacDonald resting following three concussions, Ben Blair would step up into the first team at full-back. In the absence of Mehrtens, Blair's goal-kicking was undoubtedly a contributory factor in his selection.

Elsewhere, five new caps were named, including fifth-choice hooker Andrew Hore, and scrum-half Steve Devine. For the latter, the previous three days had been eventful. The Wallaby-turned-All Black was given international clearance via the three-year residential rule after a three-day wrangle over his eligibility.

Although there was a new look to this New Zealand outfit, nobody was foolish enough to expect anything less than a tough examination of England's credentials, a fact enhanced by Mitchell's pre-match assertion. 'Like any All Black team, it's about a winning performance,' the former England assistant coach insisted. 'Nothing changes in that respect. It never will.' Taine Randell, recalled to lead the touring party, also revealed how a veritable who's who of post-war All Black captains had reminded him that fielding a weakened side would be no excuse for losing. Fred Allen, Brian Lochore, Colin Meads and Ian Kirkpatrick had all made contact. 'We were left in no doubt as to what they expected of us,' Randell reported. 'They don't care how many are resting. We are wearing the jersey and, therefore, we are expected to win.'

On the eve of the match the phrase 'vice-captain Jonny Wilkinson' was symbolic of how much had changed during the fly-half's short time in the England camp. In June 1998 the nineteen-year-old Wilkinson had received his international baptism against an Australian side which had posted 76 points against Clive Woodward's third-choice fifteen. In Dunedin a week later it was not much better. The All Blacks won 64–22, and Wilkinson was carried off in the second half as a result of a fair but crunching tackle. A year later he was substituted during a World Cup defeat at the hands of the same opponents. By his own admission, the enormity of the occasion, the intensity of the game, and the lack of time for decision-making in such a dazzling spotlight had seen the youngster freeze. 'Those games against New Zealand have certainly left a mark,' Wilkinson said. 'I use these experiences in a positive way. It provides me with a reminder of one extreme of the scale of rugby life. Hopefully that was as low as I will go.'

Captain Martin Johnson refused to be sucked into any

talk of this New Zealand team being below par. 'Lomu has always produced when it counts, and especially against us,' argued Johnson. 'His was an amazing performance in the 1995 World Cup semi-final, and his try in the 1999 World Cup group game sank us when we'd fought hard to get back into the game. It's easy to say from a broadcasting booth that Lomu's not the player he was, but they don't have to tackle him. We'll be taking him very seriously. As for the rest of the team, they are all Super 12 players, which is all you need to know.

'This is one of those must-win games, at least as far as I'm concerned. We haven't beaten them since 1993 and if we are to be taken seriously as World Cup contenders then we have to put that record right. Our World Cup preparations won't be in ruins if we lose, but we're des-

the rest of the England set-up were concerned, however, any win would do.

In the event, the win they achieved a few hours later at a packed and breathless Twickenham was earned only after one of the most entertaining and dramatic internationals

perate to beat them, not only because the All Blacks have a mystique like no other rugby team in the world, but also because it kick-starts our twelve-month build-up to the World Cup.'

On the morning of the game the pundits had England down for a comfortable win on the basis of their home advantage and the fact that they were facing a far from full-strength New Zealand team. So anything less than a convincing win and New Zealand could be seen as moral victors at least. As far as Messrs Woodward, Johnson and

witnessed at headquarters for many a year. Aficionados may have shuddered at the free-flowing scores and the sometimes less than solid defences, but the teams served up a November treat for the spectators.

The victory was inspired by Wilkinson, gaining some kind of revenge for previous mishaps with a 21-point haul that included all four methods of scoring, but this does not begin to relate the drama of the game. Trailing 31–14 after three England tries in the middle of the match, the All Blacks appeared to be on the verge of a crushing defeat.

LEFT Ben Kay's vital
last-minute line-out steal.

ABOVE Mike Tindall
begins a massive eight
months in his
international career.

Only a bone-shuddering tackle by Ben Cohen in the closing moments and a towering catch by Ben Kay, stolen at an All Black line-out on his own line, prevented this supposedly second-string New Zealand side achieving one of the greatest comebacks ever. In the end England did just enough to break their All Black hoodoo and record their fifth win in ninety-seven years of playing New Zealand. In doing so they had to thank, in particular, Johnson, Cohen, and a Wilkinson clearly inspired by his promotion to vice-

captain. He had to be, too, to counter a motivated Lomu wounded by his coach's cutting remarks earlier in the week.

It took Lomu only two touches of the ball to make his mark. England's nemesis over the years had already sent Wilkinson flying with his first surge when, in the 15th minute, he rewarded his side's bravery for refusing a penalty kick at the posts by ducking low and bulldozing through both Jason Robinson and Mike Tindall to touch down in the corner. The try, and Blair's subsequent conversion, nudged New Zealand 7–6 ahead after two previous Wilkinson penalties, and served notice that, under-strength or not, this was still a side teeming with talent and

determination. When Wilkinson slotted home a 28th-minute drop-goal, however, the majority of the Twickenham crowd expected experience to start telling.

Instead New Zealand hit back five minutes later when Tana Umaga intercepted Richard Hill's pass, fed Doug Howlett and watched as the winger sprinted forty metres to score under the posts. This was the Northern Hemisphere's first live glimpse of the man who had earned a glowing reputation during the Tri-Nations. After outsprinting Jason Robinson, no less, it was obvious that the rumours were true.

Specialist coach Phil Larder had developed one of the meanest defences in world rugby, and England were unaccustomed to conceding tries like this, especially at Twickenham. Nevertheless, having been asked a question, they delivered the perfect answer.

It began modestly enough with Wilkinson's third penalty, two minutes before the break. Then possibly the crucial score of the whole game occurred in the fourth minute of first-half injury time. Up to this point both Lewis Moody and James Simpson-Daniel had been given little chance to shine, but they, together with Wilkinson, would combine to score England's first try and provide an unexpected interval lead. It was Wilkinson's decision to take a Lomu hit that provided Simpson-Daniel, as ever with devastating speed off the mark, with enough space to exploit. Sucking in the remaining All Black defence, he fed Moody, lurking on the wing, with half a metre of room to dive into the corner. The flanker bravely plunged through two tackles to score.

'It was a classic case of three against two,' Moody explained. 'When I received the ball I knew I was going to score, but I also knew it was going to hurt because I was aware of two big guys coming at me. As I touched down one landed on my shoulder, and the other's knee punched into my kidney. As I lay on the ground I practically threw up. It was a dream come true, though, to score a try against the team I had always fantasised about playing against.'

England returned to the dressing-room at 17–14 with an ideal launchpad to wreak what would prove to be early second-half havoc. During the interval Will Greenwood retired with a dead leg, signalling an unexpected call-up for Saracens centre Ben Johnston. Losing a player of Greenwood's craft and guile could have been a major blow to England. Instead, they were about to hit an astonishing purple patch.

Five minutes into the second half Wilkinson, showing a maverick streak to add to his many other qualities at stand-off, bamboozled the flat All Blacks defence by chipping over debutant hooker Hore, then beating substitute scrum-half Danny Lee, on for the injured Devine, to touch down. It was a virtuoso try out of nothing, a triumph of perception and precision. It also provided some significant daylight between the teams for the first time in the game.

'I think there are areas of my personality that have been lying dormant while I have been growing used first to professional and then to international rugby,' said Wilkinson later, explaining his sudden impetuosity. 'Now it's fair to say that the maverick is beginning to come out of the closet. It's all to do with having thirty-five caps to my name and being part of the England set-up now for four years. I've grown in experience and confidence. I'm beginning to make better decisions, and that's partly down to attitude. I've become more realistic. I may make what turns out to be the wrong decision, but at the time I believe it to be the correct one.

More was to come. Just two minutes later Wilkinson's clever flick sent Ben Cohen clear. The strapping winger still had plenty of work to do, but his rare combination of strength and speed saw him burst through the gaps in the retreating New Zealand defence and score from forty metres. This was probably his most impressive try to date, revealing an extra gear acquired over the summer to compliment his power. Cohen clearly thought this, too, judg-

LEFT An airborne Robinson clutches
a high bomb from the All Blacks.

BELOW Quick service from Matt Dawson.

ing by the extravagant swallow dive he performed before grounding the ball. He was later criticised in some quarters for his celebration, although the dive produced one of the more memorable photographs of England's rugby season. 'The truth is I only dived because I was convinced Doug Howlett was right behind me,' Cohen claimed. 'Now, he's probably the fastest player in the game, so I was worried he was going to catch me. When I got close enough to dive I did, because you can't be tackled when airborne. I wasn't show-boating; it was a thought-out move to ensure the try. After that, when I kicked the ball into the crowd, all the emotions came flooding through at once and I lost it a bit.'

The try rounded off, either side of half-time, a fourteen-minute spell of twenty-two unanswered points, and as good a period of play produced by England as at any time during Woodward's five years in charge. With the England pack seemingly in charge, too, the Twickenham crowd and Sky Television viewers sat back to enjoy what was looking like a record romp. It appeared to be game over to every-one except New Zealand and, in particular, a certain Polynesian winger. Not content with barging his huge hulk past two players to score in the first half, Lomu helped himself to a second try, this time running through chal-lenges from Tindall, Cohen, Robinson and Johnston, who were all clinging on to the winger like terriers. With replacement stand-off Mehrtens, on for the injured Spencer at half-time, converting, New Zealand found themselves ten points in arrears and with renewed confidence. 'Lomu made me look like an idiot,' admitted Mike Tindall, referring to his efforts to halt the human juggernaut. 'Mind you, he's done that to quite a few players before me, and he'll continue to do so to quite a few after me as well.' James Simpson-Daniel, meanwhile, said: 'I was certain he'd have a huge game. It was a very different Jonah to the one I first met against the Barbarians.'

The All Blacks sensed the game was far from over. 'The key for us was not to be startled by England's lead,' the New Zealand captain, Taine Randell, would explain an hour later. 'The worst thing would have been for us to have gone off our heads.'

There was little chance of this. The All Blacks began to press hard as England defended for all their worth. Phil Vickery had already suffered the ignominy of being splattered by a Lomu challenge – and not many players can do that to a man of Vickery's size and strength – but the big Cornish prop made amends when he pulled off one of the tackles of the afternoon to prevent a certain try for his opposing prop, Joe McDonnell.

On the meeting with Lomu, the England tighthead had plenty to say. 'I wasn't expecting to be tackling him at all at that moment,' he explained. 'In fact, I was heading towards the corner flag to act as cover. I saw him bosh into two England players and run through them and fully expected him to carry on down the blindside but, at the last moment, he suddenly turned and veered straight at me. He's a very big, very strong man, but it didn't help that I had both feet planted on the ground and was not balanced correctly when he dipped his shoulder and ran at me. I went straight over on to my back, and I shot straight up again to my feet to try to make out it didn't hurt. At my club, Gloucester, our French prop, Patrice Collazo, told me later: "I was watching you and I like how you got up." He knew the score. I received loads of stick for it, both with England and at Gloucester.' On the McDonnell tackle, though, it was Vickery's turn to show off his strength. 'He was past me and looked to be favourite to score a try,' he recalled. 'We were really under the cosh and I just jumped at him and was able to get my whole body across to stop him. I don't think an arm would have been enough.'

New Zealand continued to look dangerous. In particular their use of decoy runners caused all kinds of confusion within the ranks of the England defence. Afterwards England would query the legitimacy of the All Black

decoys as the difference between distraction and obstruction was at times hard to discern.

With ten minutes remaining, New Zealand struck again. The reserve scrum-half, Danny Lee, managed to scamper over following Sam Broomhall's surging run and, with Mehrtens converting again, England's lead was down to just three points. With ten minutes still remaining, the All Blacks appeared to be in the box seat to complete the job. England, after all, were losing on the try count by four to three, and had conceded more tries in one afternoon than they had throughout the previous season's Six Nations tournament. New Zealand were not interested in anything less than a win. In the remaining time they did not once work themselves into a position for Mehrtens to attempt a drop goal to tie. It was, as far as the All Blacks were concerned, win or bust.

England managed to hang on mainly because of two late, late moments of high drama. First came Ben Cohen's tackle on Ben Blair. In a typically flowing downfield move, Howlett first drew Jason Robinson and then sent Blair sprinting clear along the touchline under the West Stand with nobody between him and the line. Cohen had some ground to make up as he tracked across from the blindside wing in the role of auxiliary full-back, but he managed to collar the Kiwi winger just a couple of metres from the corner flag. The crashing tackle was timed to perfection and sent Blair flying into touch. It was probably the cover tackle of Cohen's career, although the Northampton winger was under no illusions over the repercussions should he have missed. 'It's my job to do that. I wouldn't have played for England again if I hadn't made that tackle,' a relieved Cohen admitted afterwards. 'I'd have packed my bags and gone straight home.' The manner in which Cohen took out Blair underlined the speed of decision-making required in international rugby. 'I had to weigh up the situation,' Cohen explained. 'How quick is Blair? Can he beat me to the corner? Will he step inside me? By slowing up I'd show him the outside but prevent him from stepping inside. But the risk was that by slowing up too much he'd beat me to the corner. Anyway, I slowed, he went for the corner, and then I had to go for broke to make it.

Having reached him, I had to hit him high, because he would have dived over if I'd taken out just his legs.'

Then, with just seconds remaining on referee Jonathan Kaplan's watch, and with the tension almost unbearable, came Ben Kay's timely intervention. The All Black line-out a metre from England's line came about after Robinson, under pressure from the quicksilver Howlett, slid out of touch on all fours. Kay, the Leicester lock on for Danny Grewcock after an hour of this pulsating game, stole possession after a colossal leap to grab the ball from under the All Blacks' noses. The moment contained echoes of Justin Harrison's last-minute steal for the Wallabies in the final, winning, test against the British and Irish Lions back in 2001. Man-of-the-match Wilkinson punted the ball to safety from behind his own line seconds before the final whistle and the subsequent scenes of jubilation from the England team, bench and management.

A relieved Clive Woodward had accomplished his mission, even if it had become too tense for comfort towards the end. 'We got what we wanted out of this game and this was a win,' he said. Bearing in mind England's track record against New Zealand, he could not really have asked for any more. The England Head Coach was full of praise for Lomu: 'He's still a world-class player and a big-match one, too. We lost him a couple of times and he made us pay for it.'

Looking ahead to England's second international the following week against Australia, Woodward accepted that there were areas that needed improving: 'We're going to be very self-critical in preparing for Australia. Today we were very good for half an hour and below standard for fifty minutes. As a result, it could have gone either way.'

Indeed it could, although the bottom line was that England had seen off their bogey team, maintained their daunting home record at Twickenham, and laid the foundation to what could prove to be a remarkable autumn series.

Next up, the world champions.

ENGLAND 32

AUSTRALIA 31

Saturday, 16 November 2002 at Twickenham

ENGLAND

Robinson, Simpson-Daniel, Greenwood, Tindall (Healey, 83), Cohen, Wilkinson, Dawson, Leonard, Thompson, Vickery, Johnson, Kay, Moody, Back, Hill (Dallaglio, 41–51)

SUBS (not used): Regan, Morris, Grewcock, Gomarsall, Stimpson

Tries
Cohen 2
Conversions
Wilkinson 2
Penalties
Wilkinson 6

AUSTRALIA

Burke, Sailor, Herbert (Giteau, 73), Flatley, Mortlock, Larkham, Gregan, Young, Paul (Freier, 69), Noriega (Farwin, 77), Vickerman (Giffin, 56), Harrison (Croft, 56), Cockbain, Smith, Kefu

SUBS (not used): Whitaker, Staniforth

Tries
Flatley 2, Sailor
Conversions
Burke 2
Penalties
Burke 4

Referee
Paul Honiss (New Zealand)

Attendance
75,000

CHAPTER TWO

'They say Twickenham is a quiet place, but today it was brilliant'

W hile England were fending off New Zealand at Twickenham the current world and Tri-Nations champions were producing a sorry display against a fired-up Ireland at Lansdowne Road. It was the Wallabies first defeat in Dublin since 1968, and they were unable to conjure up even a single try. This was perhaps the most surprising match in a weekend which had seen New Zealand going down at Twickenham, and South Africa losing in Paris, three results which amounted to a rare and emphatic triumph for the Northern Hemisphere over the Southern.

LEFT Practice makes perfect: Jonny Wilkinson's familiar narrow-angle routine.

RIGHT Ben Cohen enjoying a momentous autumn series.

patrolling the gates. With captain George Gregan temporarily out of the country, vice-captain Matt Burke oversaw the proceedings, a task he performed much to coach Eddie Jones's satisfaction. 'Standing up in small groups and discussing what needs to be done before we take on England clears the mind,' Jones explained. 'We all know that our performance against Ireland wasn't good enough.'

Gregan's absence was due to the birth of his second child back in Sydney. Less than two hours after traipsing off the Lansdowne Road grass, Gregan had boarded a London-bound flight which then connected to Sydney via Singapore. He spent the whole of the Sunday flying, arriving in Australia at dawn on the Monday. His daughter was born on the Tuesday, with Gregan leaving that night for the long-haul return trip to London. Amazingly, four hours after arriving at Heathrow Airport on the Wednesday morning, Gregan was coaching children in Richmond-upon-Thames. In total, the world's most capped scrum-half had travelled 21,400 miles and through twenty-two time zones in three and a half days to see the birth of his child *and* win his eightieth international cap later in the same week. Eddie Jones had no doubts about his captain's stamina, however. 'George is a resilient character,' he said. 'We fully support his decision to go home. These are special occasions that don't come along very often. It would be difficult if it didn't involve someone with George's professionalism. He is our foremost leader, the fulcrum of everything we do, a world-class player and an outstanding captain.'

If Gregan was the talking point on the Monday, there was no doubt who created most of the interest twenty-four hours later. Clive Woodward's team selections were always eagerly anticipated, if only because he regularly came up with something new. This time, all the attention fell on Lawrence Dallaglio, who found himself dropped to the bench for the first time in seven years. Rather than enjoying the privilege of leading England out in recognition of winning his fiftieth cap, Dallaglio would be one of the seven reserves. It was a further reminder from Woodward, after his dropping of Neil Back the previous week, that reputations counted for nothing any more. 'We pick on what we see, not reputation,' explained the England Head Coach. 'Hopefully Lawrence will be a very

Predictably, the response Down Under to Australia's shock reverse was scathing. *The Australian* newspaper referred to the team as 'wretched Wallabies', the performance as an 'error-riddled embarrassment', and the game as a whole as 'a tryless shocker'. Over in England the reaction to Australia's setback was guarded. Perhaps the Wallabies were simply not good enough, which would be welcome news for Clive Woodward and his men. Alternatively, it might just have been a bad day at the office from a ring-rusty team. In which case the wounded Australians would be looking to make their next opponents pay. Either way, the Cook Cup clash was set up very nicely indeed. Having lost for two consecutive years against England in this annual autumn meeting – first to Dan Luger's dramatic, injury-time winning try in 2000, and then to the unerring accuracy of Jonny Wilkinson's left boot – Australia were even more keen than usual to secure a win.

Hence there was a day of soul-searching and home truths in London on the Monday, when the Wallabies chose to train indoors at the Wellington Barracks with armed Scots Guards

angry young man. You have to be brutally honest with players, but this is by no means the end for him. I know he'll be back and we'll get the same fantastic reaction as we did from Back. No spitting of the dummy is expected with Lawrence.'

Dallaglio found himself alongside fellow Lion Danny Grewcock on the bench, providing further evidence that the second and back rows in the England squad are the most competitive units of all. Ben Kay, with his last-minute line-out steal, and Back had both made big enough second-half impressions as substitutes against New Zealand to warrant a starting place a week later. In the latter's case, other changes had to be made to accommodate him. Thus Richard Hill, switched from number six to seven the previous week, was now moved from seven to eight, while Lewis Moody's starring role against the All Blacks ensured his retention at six.

Dallaglio, unsurprisingly, reacted to the shock of losing his place in the manner everyone expected of him. 'If you have a quiet game in attack, which I had, the coaches are going to look at the options,' he conceded. 'It is a reminder that only those playing at their best will get into the England team. A setback like this makes you much more determined to overcome it. I have to ensure I work on my game, do whatever it takes to get back into the team and come back stronger. Rest assured, I'm already doing it.' Later he would admit, 'I didn't agree with the decision, and anyone who's happy when he's dropped must have something wrong with him. It was a vote of no confidence in me and my pride was dented. But my response had to be positive.'

Lewis Moody's breaking up of what was seen as the holy trinity of back-row partnerships was no mean achievement. Such was the Leicester flanker's form that Woodward was forced to drop two former England captains in successive weeks, first Back and now Dallaglio. In just over a year Moody had progressed from third-choice openside for the Tigers, where he was battling against Back and Josh Kronfeld, to first-choice blindside for England. It was a personal triumph for the twenty-four-year-old, who had stayed at Leicester in spite of many offers from other Premiership clubs, preferring to fight his corner even though he was up against two giants in the history of the back row.

'You always get the same performance from Lewis,' said assistant coach Andy Robinson. 'His pace, handling skills and raw courage are all top drawer. He only knows one way to go, and that's forward. As far as I'm concerned, he's A1.'

Moody himself was understandably relieved by his selection. 'To retain my place had been my main goal,' he said. 'The way I played against New Zealand must have helped, plus Lawrence had, for him, a quiet game. I wasn't surprised that Neil's back in. If you know the character of the man, you know that he won't give up his international career until he wants to. His mental approach is spot on. It's no longer a battle against his size for him, but against his age.'

The young flanker's shoulder, however, hurt when scoring against the All Blacks, was causing a problem or two. 'I landed on it during the team run the day before the Australia game and it hurt so much I honestly felt I'd have to pull out,' Moody revealed. 'Fortunately, on the day adrenalin hid the pain.'

When Ben Kay was selected ahead of Danny Grewcock, the response of the benched Lion epitomised the spirit in the England squad. 'I wasn't expecting to start, but Danny did tell me he was a little worried about his place after the New Zealand game,' Kay explained. 'When I got the nod, Danny was the first person to congratulate me. You expect that kind of attitude now in the England team because that's the mentality that has been built up, plus the role of the reserve on the bench has far more importance than it ever used to have. That said, though, Danny's the kind of guy who would take this attitude no matter where he was.

'As he had played in the second row for the Lions against Australia during the 2001 tour Down Under, he made a point on sitting down with me and working through the line-outs and their players. You may think that's strange coming from a guy who had just lost his place to me, but that's the character Danny is.'

The selection of Ben Cohen on the wing would not have surprised anyone, but the news was greeted with a surge of emotion and relief by the Northampton player himself. Two years previously he had withdrawn from the England side to face Australia after hearing of his father's death. Peter Cohen was beaten up outside his Northampton nightclub and later died from a heart-attack believed to have been brought on by

his injuries. A year later, after a disappointing Lions tour, Cohen could only make the bench for the return fixture, and failed to come on to the field.

'Australia was the big game for me because of all that had happened,' Cohen explained. 'I'd never played against them but would have done had it not been for my father's death. That chance was taken away from me. After the All Blacks game I spent an anxious couple of days waiting for the announcement of the England team to face Australia. I didn't tell Clive Woodward because I didn't want him to be concerned about my emotional state. I kept my thoughts to myself but I was very relieved when I saw I got the nod. I'd been given the chance to lay a ghost to rest.'

In a poignant reaction to his selection, Cohen took a trip on his day off forty-eight hours before the game to the Northampton graveyard where his father is buried. There he placed a laminated photograph of his swallow dive against the All Blacks on the gravestone with a simple message: 'Dad: This one is for you.' Rugby had proved to be Cohen's release from the family trauma caused by his father's death and subsequent trial. Now he finally had the chance to show the Australians what he could do. 'It was the second anniversary of my father's death,' Cohen said. 'I find it very difficult to visit him at his grave, but this time I just had to do it. My dad would have loved seeing me score that try and would have loved having the photograph next to him.'

On the Wednesday Australia named their team to face England. After a turgid win in Argentina and then the sorry defeat in Dublin, changes were inevitable, and there were five alterations to the team who lost to Ireland. Four of those were in the tight five: Jeremy Paul and Bill Young returned to the front row as hooker and loosehead respectively, with Dan Vickerman and Justin Harrison in the lock positions ahead of David Giffin and the injured Owen Finegan. With the likes of Gregan, Stephen Larkham, Daniel Herbert, Matt Burke and the former rugby league star Wendell Sailor in the backs, the Wallabies would clearly pose a major threat, regardless of recent form. This was a heavyweight outfit.

Furthermore, England's preparation was disrupted late on. At the age of thirty-four Jason Leonard was promoted back into the starting fifteen to win his ninety-eighth cap in place of Gloucester's Trevor Woodman, who withdrew after a neck

RIGHT Simpson-Daniel in action against Australia, unaware that he is suffering from glandular fever.

injury sustained against New Zealand failed to heal. Northampton's Robbie Morris, at just twenty years of age, would take Leonard's place on the bench.

While Martin Johnson had been captain only for the one test against New Zealand, most assumed that he would be reappointed for the remainder of the autumn series. With the victory against the All Blacks under his belt, whatever lingering doubt there may have been disappeared entirely. Against Australia, in what proved to be a thriller every bit as pulsating as the high-scoring encounter the week before at Twickenham, captain Johnson would make his mark in a vital fashion.

Although not one for tub-thumping rhetoric, the England captain has often uttered the right sentence at the right time. Colleagues talk of the first time England played at a passionate Millennium Stadium, for example, when an incredibly partisan crowd at their vocal best awaited England's arrival on to the field. Johnson halted his men moments before emerging from the players' tunnel and gave them one final order: 'Let's silence *that*,' he said. After

a quarter of an hour England were two tries to the good and the crowd was hushed. Against Australia Johnson had to find even better words.

Enjoying a ten-point lead close to half-time, England were hit by a triple burst of Wallaby tries in the space of nine frantic minutes either side of the interval. Suddenly Johnson's team were twelve points down against the world champions. The impregnable home record, unblemished since that World

Cup defeat to New Zealand way back in 1999, was under serious threat, as were England's World Cup credentials. Losing at home to Australia would be no disgrace, but it would hardly bolster England's argument that they were on course to win the greatest honour in the game.

Then came Johnson's moment of inspiration. Gathering his beleaguered men underneath the posts in a huddle while Matt Burke prepared to convert Australia's third try, the big lock delivered a simple statement: 'This is what great teams are made of,' he said. 'To come back from this.'

The fact that they then achieved the comeback was impressive enough. But the manner in which they reached their goal left the greater mark. There was no blind panic. No frantic hurling of the ball. No lucky breaks. Coolly and calmly, England ate away at the Wallaby lead through Wilkinson's trusty left boot, before Cohen scored his second try of the game and Wilkinson's conversion edged England into a one-point lead.

There was still a final scare for England, though. Australia were awarded a penalty five minutes before the end of the match when England were judged to be offside. Burke stepped up to take the kick, which was certainly kickable, but the pressure told and the ball sailed a few inches wide of the upright.

So England won their third Cook Cup in a row, and in the process secured their seventh straight win over the Tri-Nations teams. It was the longest spell of dominance over both

ABOVE Cohen scores his first try of the game against Australia.

Australia and the whole Southern Hemisphere in the history of international rugby.

After such a stirring performance it is always difficult to pick out individuals, but Cohen and Wilkinson were two world-class players at their peak. Cohen's two tries, his seventeenth and eighteenth in just his nineteenth international, enhanced his fast-growing reputation on the international stage, and maintained his superb run of form after the previous week's virtuoso try against the All Blacks. Having performed his swallow dive seven days before, Cohen produced another memorable image after his second-half try when he cocked his hand to his ear to hear the response from an ecstatic English crowd. 'I just thought that the crowd were really getting their money's worth,' he said. 'It was cracking value for money, and I wanted to hear them.' This, predictably, made

most of the newspaper back pages the following morning. Wilkinson, meanwhile, notched up twenty-two points: six penalties and two conversions. Not for the first time, the Newcastle Falcons stand-off hit perfection, scoring with every kick he attempted. And it wasn't as if they were all sitters: several were from fifty metres out or more. Add to this the fact that each time he stepped up he did so with the knowledge that one miss at this level could cost England the match and one can imagine the pressure.

Wilkinson's display prompted England's defensive coach, Phil Larder, one not normally given to eulogise, to say: 'Jonny will be talked about in a hundred years' time. He's a great player. A superstar.' Clearly others felt the same because, even before the game had started, Wilkinson had learned that he had been voted the International Players' Player of the Year. His performance against Australia more than justified this latest award.

Early in the game, however, there was little to suggest that England would be required to regroup and produce such an impressive comeback. After Burke missed a penalty, England forged ahead. Jason Robinson came into the line to make an extra man, James Simpson-Daniel took out three Australian defenders with a jinking run to open the gap for Cohen to collect, score and provide the photo-opportunity for the waiting press. With Wilkinson converting, it was the perfect start for an England team keen to begin positively after their desperate survival the week before against the All Blacks. The pressurised Wallabies clawed their way back with two Burke penalties, only for Wilkinson to increase England's advantage with a monstrous penalty from well inside his own half. When he then struck two more, England had eased into a 16–6 lead and appeared poised to produce their usual second-half onslaught.

Australia, as befitting world champions, had other ideas. Physical in approach, and hell-bent on nailing both Wilkinson and Robinson early, the Wallabies launched a series of attacks as the first half entered injury time. Twice Gregan, revealing no signs of tiredness despite his round-the-world excursion, refused simple penalty kicks at the posts in favour of scrums. To have scored three points from one of these chances would have left his side just a converted try behind at the break, but Gregan wanted more. If Australia had gained no return for their endeavour before the whistle they might well have entered their dressing-room in dispirited mood. But Elton Flatley, playing at inside centre but often sharing the role of stand-off with Stephen Larkham, took full advantage of a Wilkinson slip to burst through the gap between

ABOVE Wilkinson on his way to kicking twenty-two points.

England's number ten and Will Greenwood to score and leave Burke with an easy conversion. Despite his personal haul of points, Wilkinson was mortified by his error: 'I fell flat on my face for the Flatley try at the worst possible moment,' he later admitted. 'It disappointed me massively, and made me annoyed with myself.'

The score clearly lifted the Wallabies, now just three points in arrears and worse was to befall England three minutes into the second half. Larkham exploited another gap in the home defence to break through before sending a long, looping pass across to the right wing where a waiting Wendell Sailor barged past Cohen to score his first try on his fifth international appearance since switching codes twelve months before. For Sailor, formerly the superstar of Australian rugby league, this was a moment of triumph after enduring constant and rather unfair criticism for his failure to make an immediate impact in international rugby union.

England responded by surging into the Australian twenty-two but could then only watch in despair as Flatley, scooping up a ball that had squirted loose from a ruck close to the Wallaby line, sprinted a full eighty metres and evaded the despairing dive of Robinson to touch down close enough to the posts for Burke to convert.

From ten points up, England were trailing by twelve in the space of nine astonishing minutes. Suddenly they were contemplating the end of a sixteen-match unbeaten run at Twickenham. For Richard Hill especially, the transformation of the game had been unbelievable. When he left the pitch for stitches in a wound on the bridge of his nose, England were winning 16–13. When he returned, they were losing 28–16. 'There was a television in the stitch room so I was aware that Australia were putting us under huge pressure,' he explained.

'But when I went back on I didn't know the score, and had no idea that Australia had completely swung the match round.'

It was an interesting experience for Dallaglio, too, who won his fiftieth cap when replacing Hill for those damaging ten minutes. 'Reaching fifty was completely lost on the day but I didn't lose any sleep over it,' he said. 'It was disappointing, of course, but I've had the honour of leading England out on a number of occasions before. As I came off the pitch this time someone shouted from the crowd: "Oi, Dallaglio, we've just conceded fifteen points with you on."'

Then came Johnson's pep talk under the posts. A couple of years before, maybe even twelve months previously, the response would have been frenetic. It might have worked, or it could well have let in the opposition for more points. This time, England knew there was still time to claw their

BELOW Cohen's second try set up Wilkinson's winning conversion but, according to Will Greenwood, it could have been nearer the posts.

RIGHT Jonny Wilkinson directing proceedings from stand off; Martin Johnson lifts the Cook Cup for a third successive time.

Simpson-Daniel, a test-match debutant only the week before, created space to release Cohen. The left wing, enjoying the form of his life, still had plenty of work to do but his strength and speed saw off both Gregan and Larkham. 'I was mindful to come inside from the wing and look for some work,' Cohen explained, reliving his try. 'I remember shouting out at Simpson-Daniel that I'd be coming short off him. As a result, I hit a hole where George Gregan should have been, and I was through. When I touched down Will Greenwood was the first

way back, even though it had to be done against the world champions.

'If we'd gone for the big plays, it would have been suicide against a team like Australia,' Phil Larder argued later. He was right. This was a time for patience and practice, which is easily said but not so easily carried out in the face of such pressure.

Wilkinson and Burke swapped penalties before two further strikes from the England stand-off not only raised his side's morale but, more crucially, reduced the arrears to six points. Now it was the turn of the Wallabies to feel the pressure as the crowd sensed the momentum was back with Clive Woodward's men. With thirteen minutes remaining,

to reach me. I thought he was going to congratulate me, but instead he said: "Great try, but you could have got closer to the posts." Even though it was an incredibly important moment in the game, and Jonny still had to kick what would prove to be the winning conversion, it made me laugh out loud.'

With Wilkinson's conversion, and Burke's subsequent miss, England won for the second week running by the narrowest of margins, and in some style.

Woodward was understandably delighted with both the result and his team's performance. 'The character in my team is fantastic,' the England Head Coach said on Saturday evening. 'We dug ourselves a huge hole and we'd all but blown

but made a salient point concerning home advantage: 'England have become virtually unbeatable at Twickenham and technically very good. But their big test will come away from home. Then we'll see how good they are. Home advantage has increasing importance in the world game. The top ten teams in international rugby win seventy-seven per cent of home matches and there is a fifteen per cent differential in penalties for the home team over the away team. Two years ago we were winning the kind of game you've just seen. Now we're losing them. England are very mature. They know how to win games but home advantage is a big factor and the World Cup will be at neutral venues. In Australia!'

Jason Leonard, England's sole survivor from the team beaten by Australia in the 1991 World Cup final at Twickenham, agreed with Jones's assessment. 'This is a great win for us but

it. But we showed the strength to bounce back against the world champions. I'm sure everyone who was here felt privileged to have seen such a great game of rugby. You have to applaud every player involved, including the Australians. It was a great spectacle and the atmosphere was fantastic. They say Twickenham is a quiet place, but today it was brilliant.

'The whole dressing-room is elated, not only by the result but by the nature in which we achieved it. I was always convinced that we could come back. We just had to get the message out to them, to calm down when we went 31–19 behind, because there was still time.'

The Australian coach Eddie Jones was gracious in defeat,

we were on our home turf,' the NEC Harlequins prop said. 'The true test of the side will come when we're on tour Down Under next summer.'

The lessons from this dramatic win would undoubtedly be valuable come the World Cup. 'We'll know what we'll be up against and we'll be used to coping with the pressure,' insisted Ben Cohen. 'But we'll go to the World Cup believing we can win it,' added Wilkinson.

Such was the confidence after this stunning win. Now only South Africa stood between England and a unique Southern Hemisphere treble that would consolidate England's status among the world's elite.

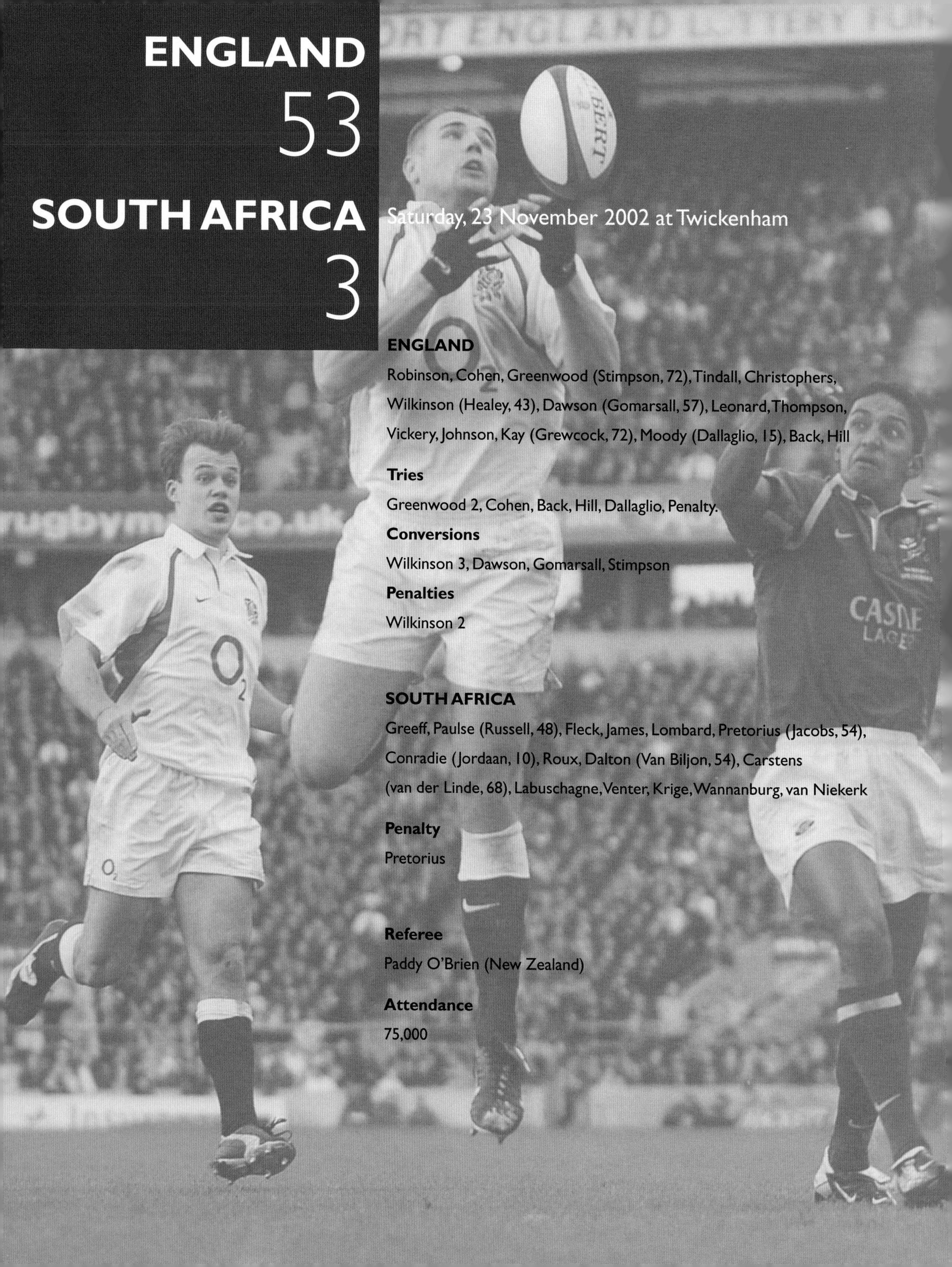

ENGLAND 53
SOUTH AFRICA 3

Saturday, 23 November 2002 at Twickenham

ENGLAND

Robinson, Cohen, Greenwood (Stimpson, 72), Tindall, Christophers, Wilkinson (Healey, 43), Dawson (Gomarsall, 57), Leonard, Thompson, Vickery, Johnson, Kay (Grewcock, 72), Moody (Dallaglio, 15), Back, Hill

Tries

Greenwood 2, Cohen, Back, Hill, Dallaglio, Penalty.

Conversions

Wilkinson 3, Dawson, Gomarsall, Stimpson

Penalties

Wilkinson 2

SOUTH AFRICA

Greeff, Paulse (Russell, 48), Fleck, James, Lombard, Pretorius (Jacobs, 54), Conradie (Jordaan, 10), Roux, Dalton (Van Biljon, 54), Carstens (van der Linde, 68), Labuschagne, Venter, Krige, Wannanburg, van Niekerk

Penalty

Pretorius

Referee

Paddy O'Brien (New Zealand)

Attendance

75,000

CHAPTER THREE

'We have always been the team everyone wants to beat'

And so to the final leg of this epic trilogy against the full force of the Southern Hemisphere, and a test match that would spawn not only a record score but scenes of brutality rarely witnessed at headquarters. Such were the assaults committed on the pitch that what should have been a triumphant celebration of English rugby was marred. The inquests into what had occurred would rage on for many weeks afterwards.

Like Australia the week before, South Africa faced England under severe pressure after a disastrous tour of the Northern Hemisphere to date. Losing by a record margin in Paris, while difficult to accept, could be rationalised by the fact that it came at the hands of the 2002 Six Nations champions and serious contenders for the World Cup the following year. Losing by another record margin in Scotland the week after, however, was beyond the pale.

The Springbok coach, Rudi Straeuli, arrived in London intent on trying out as many players as possible. Having made ten changes between Paris and Edinburgh, the former

Nevertheless, the team he would be announcing later in the week to play England would bear no resemblance to that which finished the Tri-Nations by beating Australia and losing narrowly to New Zealand. 'I have been hired to win the World Cup for South Africa and if I have to play people to give them experience, that's what I will do,' he insisted. 'You've got to teach them about rugby. That means they have to experience life at international level. I can't do it for them. But make no mistake, in South Africa we have the players for the game plan.'

England's plans, meanwhile, were hit even before Clive

Bedford coach hinted at many more for their Twickenham encounter. 'A rugby team consists of fifteen players,' he argued. 'So you can only make fifteen changes.'

The World Cup winner in 1995 had come to Europe with one eye on the 2003 renewal of that tournament. With ten or more established players rehabilitating from injury at home, Straeuli was prepared for a tough baptism on this short autumn tour, although he had not prepared himself for losing to France and Scotland by an aggregate of thirty-five points.

Woodward could announce his team on the Monday night. James Simpson-Daniel revealed that he was suffering from glandular fever and was sent home to his family in Cleveland to convalesce. Trevor Woodman also had to withdraw, still suffering from his neck injury.

Simpson-Daniel's illness was a major blow for the twenty-year-old Gloucester wing. His impressive performance against the Wallabies became more commendable when it was discovered that he'd been suffering with the illness during that match. He would be out of action until at least the turn of the year, ending the debate for the time being over whether his best position for his country was on the wing or at centre. 'Just when I've got my confidence up I get shot down by some-

ried me through. But as soon as the game against the Wallabies was over I felt unbelievably rough. It was as if I was on a different planet. I felt totally exhausted. When I managed to meet my family after the game they all told me how awful

ABOVE Will Greenwood winds and weaves his way to the first of two tries.

LEFT Line-out practice before the battle with the Boks.

thing that seems pathetic,' he lamented. 'I'm so angry. I was still hoping for a big game against South Africa and all of a sudden I won't be there. I felt ill the morning after the New Zealand game, sweating through the night and having headaches. I thought it was just nerves and the adrenalin car-

I looked. I should have been enjoying the fact that I'd just won my first two caps for England and won both games at Twickenham against New Zealand and Australia, but I was far too ill to appreciate it. It was massively tough to miss out on South Africa. I was absolutely desperate to play, but to miss out with something totally unrelated to rugby was gutting.'

Although Austin Healey appeared to be the favourite to take over from Simpson-Daniel, Head Coach Woodward sprung one of his frequent surprises by elevating the Bristol

wing Phil Christophers to the starting fifteen. Healey, a victim of his own versatility, was left kicking his heels again on the bench. Christophers, who had scored twice in a non-capped game against the Barbarians, and on his full debut in Argentina, had an interesting background, to say the least. Born in Germany in the old university town of Heidelberg to an English father and a German mother, his first language is German. At the age of fifteen he was selected for the German Under-19 squad, then moved to England a year later to be educated in Lancaster. A stint playing for Brive in France followed before his move to Bristol. The twenty-two-year-old

was eager to seize this unexpected opportunity. 'I'm not big on expressing my emotions to anyone,' he admitted. 'Even I have to admit, though, that it's really bizarre how a German kid has ended up playing rugby for England and fulfilling his dreams in the process. I mean, what are the odds of that happening?'

At the other end of the scale of experience, Jason Leonard had an equally interesting week. Woodman's withdrawal guaranteed the prop's inclusion in the starting fifteen for what would be his ninety-ninth international for England, although so influential had been his display against Australia that Leonard may well have received the nod in any case. As if this were not enough, Leonard completed training on the Tuesday before travelling to Buckingham Palace to receive his MBE from the Queen. 'I'd actually warned Buckingham Palace that I might have to postpone the day if Clive Woodward wanted me to attend more training,' Leonard said. 'When I asked Clive, though, he couldn't believe I should even have thought that he would prevent me. So I bundled the family into the car and drove off to Buckingham Palace in my morning suit. I didn't wear a top hat because I reckon I look ridiculous as it is without any extra help from a top hat.

'When we got there I joined a kind of Indian procession two the following morning. Apart from the return of hooker James Dalton, best known for receiving a red card for punching during the 1995 World Cup in South Africa, the major focus was on the centre pairing of Butch James and Robbie Fleck. Straeuli described this new combination as 'quite physical' (three days later, that would prove to be something of an understatement). 'I know both players are extremely motivated for Saturday's match,' the Springbok coach added. 'They enjoy attacking and they love defending.' The two big centres, renowned (if not notorious) for their past records in hard tackling, would be joining forces for the first time. They had

before finally I was called up to meet the Queen. Someone next to her explained who and what I was, she congratulated me and presented me with my medal. To be honest, I was rather embarrassed by it all because I felt undeserving. In the same room as me were people who saved lives, and all I did was play sport. I took the whole family out to lunch and, when I returned to the team hotel that evening, everyone wanted to see the MBE. They were all very happy for me, but I got the expected stick as well.'

It soon became clear that Leonard's experience would be very handy when Rudi Straeuli named his Springbok twenty-

a simple game plan: 'The only way we can beat England is to tackle them out of the game,' Fleck explained. 'We aim to operate as an aggressive defensive unit. Butch will bring an extra physical presence to the side.' James, previously at fly-half, was moved to inside centre, partly to accommodate new stand-off Andre Pretorius, but also to bolster the centre. He had not faced England the previous year as he was serving a two-month suspension for a series of late tackles against France and New Zealand….

Neil Back was secretly pleased with the Springbok team. 'As soon as I saw the fifteen I knew exactly how they would play,'

RIGHT Jason Leonard is tackled by Joe van Niekerk.

BELOW Captain Fantastic: Martin Johnson making hard yards.

he explained. 'Straight on and direct rugby. They had plenty of other players to choose from and, frankly, they might have caused us more problems if they had because hard, running rugby using the full width of the pitch is much harder to defend against.'

England's captain, Martin Johnson, was similarly under no illusions about the task facing England. 'The Springboks have always probably been the most physical side in world rugby,' he said. 'Our games against them have always been ones you remember for their toughness. If you win the physical battle, you win the game. They have a lot of pride and we'll be think-

ing about their mindset. They are a very dangerous team and, in many ways, it's going to be our toughest game of the three.'

Certainly Rudi Straeuli appeared confident, despite those setbacks in Paris and Edinburgh, when he spoke on the eve of the international. He hosted a video session for his troops featuring all of England's recent slip-ups in their attempts to claim a Grand Slam. 'England have weaknesses,' he said. 'If they didn't they wouldn't have lost at Wembley, Murrayfield, Dublin or Paris. Psychologically, we're in the right frame of mind.'

Clive Woodward expected nothing less. 'These guys are in

a corner,' he said, referring to the dangers of facing a wounded animal such as a twice-beaten Springbok. 'They will be tough and they will be physical. Nothing has changed down the decades. But if South Africa will have steam coming out of their ears, then so, too, will England. We are a tough team as well. I'm not concerned at all about foul play or the like. If we didn't have one of the top referees like Paddy O'Brien, then I might worry. But we do.'

Possibly the Head Coach's only concern centred on Jonny Wilkinson, whose tendency to get stuck in belied his size but often left the management team with their hearts in their mouths. 'If I had my way, Jonny would never go into another ruck and scrap away in the manner he does,' said Woodward. 'But that's Jonny for you. We've got a bit more out of him lately because he's not been quite as involved in all the rucks.' Little did Woodward know that by late Saturday afternoon his young star stand-off would have been very much involved through little fault of his own.

In what turned out to be one of the most savage international matches ever witnessed, England passed another crucial test. A fortnight earlier they had succeeded in holding off a late rally from New Zealand. Seven days later they had

ABOVE Wilkinson off-loads despite the attention of two Springboks.

launched a memorable comeback against Australia. Now they showed remarkable self-restraint against a South African side intent on beating England by fair and increasingly foul means. Smashing fifty-three points and seven tries past a team which for all the world seemed to be indulging in a series of pre-meditated assaults barely told the full story. The scoreline condemned the Springboks to their biggest defeat by England. It also notched up England's eighteenth straight home victory, a world record in international rugby, as well as an eighth successive win over the big three from the Southern Hemisphere and a fourth in a row against South Africa. By seeing off all three visiting countries, England also went top of the Zurich world rankings. They also gained the psychological upper hand against a team they were due to meet less than a year later in the World Cup.

However, for all the plus points for England, the match was marred from start to finish by a series of late hits, high tackles and various cheap shots from the men in green and gold. Nevertheless, the plan to shake up England, which was hardly a secret after the statements that emerged from the South African camp during the week leading up to the match, ended in abject failure and humiliation. Any number of Springboks could have been sent off, although only lock forward Jannes Labuschagne was dismissed for a 22nd-minute late, late hit on Jonny Wilkinson that pole-axed the England stand-off.

The violent tone of this conflict – for this test match *was* a conflict – was set within three minutes as Jason Robinson took a late hit and both Matt Dawson and Neil Back were on the receiving end of foul play from James Dalton and Robbie Fleck. Dalton then laid in to Steve Thompson.

It was an obvious unsettling tactic that never disturbed England. Indeed, Robbie Fleck's spat with Ben Cohen served only to move Wilkinson's first penalty ten metres nearer the posts. A little later, in the 20th minute, Matt Dawson made a typically sparkling break before feeding Cohen. The big winger then ran twenty-five metres and barged past Fleck to finish off the attack for the nineteenth try of his international career. In doing so he achieved an unprecedented feat for an English rugby player: tries against all of the world's top-ten international teams. Australia, New Zealand, France, Argentina, Ireland, Scotland, Wales and Italy had all previously felt Cohen's force. Now it was the turn of the Springboks. 'I had no idea I'd set this mark until someone told me much later,' Cohen revealed.

Any chance of South Africa recovering from this ten-point deficit evaporated two minutes later in the most abhorrent circumstances. Recognising the threat posed by Wilkinson, the Springboks were clearly intent on removing the stand-off from the fray. Labuschagne's late shoulder charge on the England number ten might have warranted a yellow card had it not been for referee O'Brien's earlier instruction to the South Africa captain, Corne Krige, to warn his players that there would be serious repercussions if the foul play continued. On seeing Labuschagne's crude challenge, O'Brien had no hesitation in giving the lock his marching orders and, in the process, handing him a little piece of unwanted history. Labuschagne became the first South African ever to be sent off at Twickenham. As he departed from the field, O'Brien had a quiet word with Martin Johnson. 'Any problems leave to me,' he said. The England captain clearly took the referee's promise on board. A few years back Johnson's one weakness in his game might have been a suspect temperament. On this day, however, he and his players refused to take the law into their hands in the face of severe provocation, revealing admirable self-control in the process.

'I don't think as a person I was particularly singled out for the rough stuff, but because the scrum-half and stand-off tend to get their hands on the ball more than any other player in the team, they are bound to be hit more,' a philosophical Wilkinson decided. 'That's why both Matt Dawson and myself suffered quite a bit in the game, added to the fact that the Springboks have always been physically the toughest of all.

'On the sending off, it wasn't being hit by Labuschagne that hurt, more the fact that I hit the ground hard from a great height. I suffered a little whiplash and was a bit dazed, too, but it was more the awkwardness of the fall.'

Wilkinson, having somewhat groggily staggered to his feet, responded by sending a cross-field punt perfectly into the path of Ben Cohen. The Northampton wing crossed the line and touched down the ball. The try, however, was disallowed after video referee Jim Fleming spotted the tiniest of knock-ons by Cohen as he jumped up to collect the high ball.

No matter. On the half-hour Will Greenwood, adopting the correct running angle, collected from twenty metres out, spun through Fleck's tackle and crashed over under the posts. 'It was a simple but clearly useful move used by the Australians previously to great effect,' Greenwood explained. 'It just needs an early call and an inside pass.' Wilkinson's conversion and later penalty kick, cancelling out a penalty from Pretorius that had broken the Springbok duck, handed England a fifteen-point lead at half-time.

This would be extended inside the first minute of the second half. Greenwood proved the tormentor again, this time throwing two dummies in a thirty-metre run that finished in the corner for a magnificent individual try. 'Mike Tindall came on a dummy switch with me which, together with Neil Back lurking outside me, allowed me to throw a dummy and open up loads of space,' the centre explained.

Soon after, England's stand-off was helped from the field with a shoulder injury. 'I passed the ball and a split-second later took a late and hard hit from James,' Wilkinson explained. 'I felt my shoulder pop almost immediately, and I knew that my game was over.' His a/c shoulder joint had been displaced, and the injury would keep him out of rugby for nine weeks. This, however, would not affect his international duties, with the Six Nations still some time away.

So South Africa had finally achieved their objective of sidelining Wilkinson, but by then the game was lost. Matt Dawson had converted Greenwood's second try while Wilkinson received treatment before he, too, left the fray after a series of batterings finally took their toll. 'They were more physical than ever, but I still thoroughly enjoyed it,' reported Dawson. 'The best way to respond was to give them a good hiding, which is exactly what we did. Our forwards have received some flak in the past for being over-physical, but their discipline was exemplary and they reacted in a very professional manner to it all.'

England still refused to retaliate, save for piling on more points. A high tackle by Greeff on Christophers as the winger headed for a score in the corner resulted in a penalty try and a simple conversion for substitute scrum-half Andy Gomarsall. Christophers admitted to apprehension even

before he was almost decapitated. 'In Argentina there wasn't much pressure on us because we were a young, inexperienced side, but before the South Africa game, where I would be winning my second cap and making my debut at Twickenham in a test match, I have never felt so nervous in my life,' he explained. 'In fact I got three cold sores just through stress.

'Everyone had warned me that the South Africans tackle harder than anyone else in the world, and they were right. I was really tired when I got the ball because I'd just spent the past few minutes doing nothing but being in contact. I saw two Springboks coming for me so I jinked inside, a movement that clearly caught Greeff by surprise. Instead of getting his full body behind the tackle, he ended up giving me the clothes line with his arm. It nearly took my head off, but didn't hurt as much as it may have looked. If it had not been for that I would have scored, but as we received the penalty try in any case I wasn't too concerned.'

Then England's celebrated back row, together again after Lawrence Dallaglio had replaced Lewis Moody in the 15th

ABOVE Phil Christophers high tackled by Werner Greeff, which led to a penalty try.

minute, all helped themselves to a try apiece. First to benefit was Neil Back, scoring one of his trademark tries in the 69th minute as England moved out of sight. The Leicester flanker emerged from the bottom of a pile of bodies with ball in hand after his drive towards the line had been supported by the full weight of the England pack. It emerged later that he had fractured his cheekbone just ten minutes into the second half but played out the match regardless. 'I don't quite know how it happened, but, although it hurt, I had no idea it was fractured until afterwards,' he said. Richard Hill then found himself on the receiving end of an Austin Healey chip across the pitch to score in the corner, although the Saracens flanker was indebted to a fortunate bounce of the ball that prevented it from finding touch. 'I'll never work out how the ball didn't bounce out,' Hill said later. Finally Dallaglio added England's seventh try in injury time, with Tim Stimpson, on for Greenwood for the final eight minutes, converting from the corner. In doing so, Stimpson became the fourth kicker to convert a try for his side in the match. That was a first in 131 years of international rugby.

The recriminations began shortly after the final whistle. 'That was a brutal test match,' said a clearly perturbed Clive Woodward. 'Wilkinson was targeted and there were green bodies smashing into my players after the ball had

ABOVE Jannes Labuschagne given his marching orders by referee Paddy O'Brien.

LEFT Ben Cohen and Robbie Fleck have a disagreement.

been passed. I'm very disappointed in the manner in which we were injured. In some cases it was nothing short of disgraceful. It was totally different to the wins over Australia and New Zealand. There was a lot going on out there, a lot of stuff off the ball. Everyone involved in rugby will have to take a look at this match again and make their own judgements.'

Woodward accepted that the bitterness resulting from such a violent test match was likely to make the forthcoming World Cup meeting between the two teams something of a grudge match. 'It just goes to show what happens when teams meet under pressure,' he continued. 'It puts down a very clear marker about what might happen in Australia next time. We're no angels, but I was proud of our self-restraint. We could have lost control but the leadership from players like Martin Johnson was superb.'

Phil Larder, not one usually fazed by physical rugby, was similarly angered by what had transpired: 'There is a line, and it is important that you don't cross it. South Africa were a mile over it.' The England players, too, had their say after the game. Although delighted with a hat-trick of wins against the

Southern Hemisphere, their joy was muted by what they had just endured. Jason Robinson, alongside Wilkinson, bore the brunt, sustaining a suspected perforated eardrum when he was taken out in an off-the-ball challenge early in the game. 'I'm really upset,' the full-back said. 'I felt it was a dirty game from the very beginning. I was hit long after the ball had been cleared. From the early stages the South Africans made their intentions clear. There were bloody noses in our team within minutes.'

Wilkinson, his right arm in a sling, summed up his mood: 'I'm very battered and I'm very bruised, but the main thing is that we scored over fifty points, didn't concede a try and refused to rise to the bait.'

Cohen, too, was taken aback by what had taken place. 'We knew South Africa were in a corner after their previous two defeats and that they would use any way possible to get out,' he said. 'We knew it would be physical and that some-one would probably get sent off. There was an awful lot of

ABOVE Neil Back celebrates after scoring a try.

sledging going on as well from the Boks. I received count-less threats about what was going to happen to me the next time I got the ball, even when they were forty points down. I think we got our point across, though, by the final score.'

Neil Back expressed his satisfaction in the way England handled the intimidation. 'We'd talked long and hard before-hand about our discipline and about not reacting,' he said. 'We're a hard team, but we've never been a dirty team and we weren't going to start going down that road against the Springboks. That's why referees like officiating England games, because we have a good rapport with them.'

The South Africans saw it all very differently, however. 'We came here as boys and we'll return as men,' insisted their coach, Rudi Straeuli, afterwards, before heightening the tension with a rather pointed jibe. 'We'll be seeing England in Perth in the World Cup. We have two players concussed and another with a dislocated shoulder, so there are a lot of incidents we could look at. Do you think we concussed ourselves?' Later, television replays from new

angles revealed not only further examples of foul play from the Springboks, but also the rather embarrassing evidence that their stand-off, Andre Pretorius, who left the fray in the second half concussed, had been accidentally struck by one of his own players.

As the final whistle shrilled around Twickenham, the South African captain, Corne Krige, had gathered his beleaguered men in a huddle. 'Remember this moment,' he told them. 'Remember how bad it feels because one year from now we will be in Perth. Remember it, because the next time England will be the ones to feel the way we do right now.'

A day later, as South Africa were preparing to return home to a national inquest, their mood had not softened. 'England are running high on confidence, but I don't rate them that much,' Krige declared. 'I think they can be taken.' Staeuli, meanwhile, defended his tactics and his team, even his red-carded lock. 'Our defensive strategy was to target someone like Wilkinson, like the French did earlier in the year when they beat the English in the Six Nations,' he said. 'But there was certainly no intention to put him off the field. Our inten-tion was to cut him off from his back line and close down his kicking options. I am happy there was no intention by Labuschagne to hurt Jonny Wilkinson.

'We are looking forward to Perth in October. I don't see it as revenge. The feeling in the dressing-room at Twickenham wasn't great, so maybe that will motivate us even more. I'm proud of the boys. Only time will tell whether we are still building to a peak or whether England have peaked too soon.'

This stance would change once the Springboks had returned home. The South African Rugby Football Union handed out fines and public reprimands to Krige, after watching replays of his numerous off-the-ball hits on unsuspecting England players, and to four of his colleagues. Straeuli, meanwhile, altered his view to the point of admitting that what had happened at Twickenham was unacceptable.

Back in England, Clive Woodward was buoyant after three wins over the big three in the Southern Hemisphere, but was also eager to keep his and his team's feet on the ground. Responding to the news that England had become the top-ranked team in the world, Woodward said: 'It's a source of satisfaction but, in reality, Australia are number one because they won the last World Cup.' On the autumn tests, though, the England Head Coach was delighted with the progress that had been made. 'We are a better team than we were three weeks ago and I am perfectly happy that England will arrive at the World Cup with a strong squad of players who can really enjoy the tournament. I don't necessarily want the respect of the Southern Hemisphere. The more they throw at us, the more they are worried about us. We have always been the team everyone wants to beat.'

***

The unprecedented hat-trick of wins over such illustrious opponents had been the perfect start to the England national team's season. It laid the foundation for another tilt at the Six Nations and a Grand Slam. For many of the more senior players, the forthcoming Six Nations could well be their last taste of the tournament that is the envy of the rest of the rugby world. It had been good to Clive Woodward's men insofar as titles had been won, together with Triple Crowns, and Calcutta Cups. But it had also been a source of torment for a team which had evolved together over the previous five years. For all of England's success during this period, and for all their stunning rugby, they were still best noted for letting slip not one, but three Grand Slams on the last weekend of the tournament. Those shock defeats – to Wales at Wembley, Scotland in the sleet and cold of Murrayfield, and finally Ireland in the foot-and-mouth-delayed international at Lansdowne Road –

ABOVE The ball's in there somewhere – a second try for the free-scoring Greenwood.

ABOVE RIGHT Wilkinson's battered shoulder gives way.

RIGHT Phil Vickery lunges through Corne Krige's tackle.

had raised serious questions over whether England had the character to see a job through to its conclusion.

Impossible to beat at Twickenham for years, England were a different proposition away from home, as France exploited when deservedly beating them at the Stade de France on their way to claiming the 2002 Grand Slam. For England, the ultimate accolade in Northern Hemisphere rugby had eluded them since 1995, a full two years before Clive Woodward had taken over the reins.

If there was ever a time to put this right, it would be in 2003, before the old guard retired, and before England journeyed to Australia to contend the World Cup. With a Grand Slam under their belts, they could travel with hope and confidence. Without one, few would rate England's chances to go

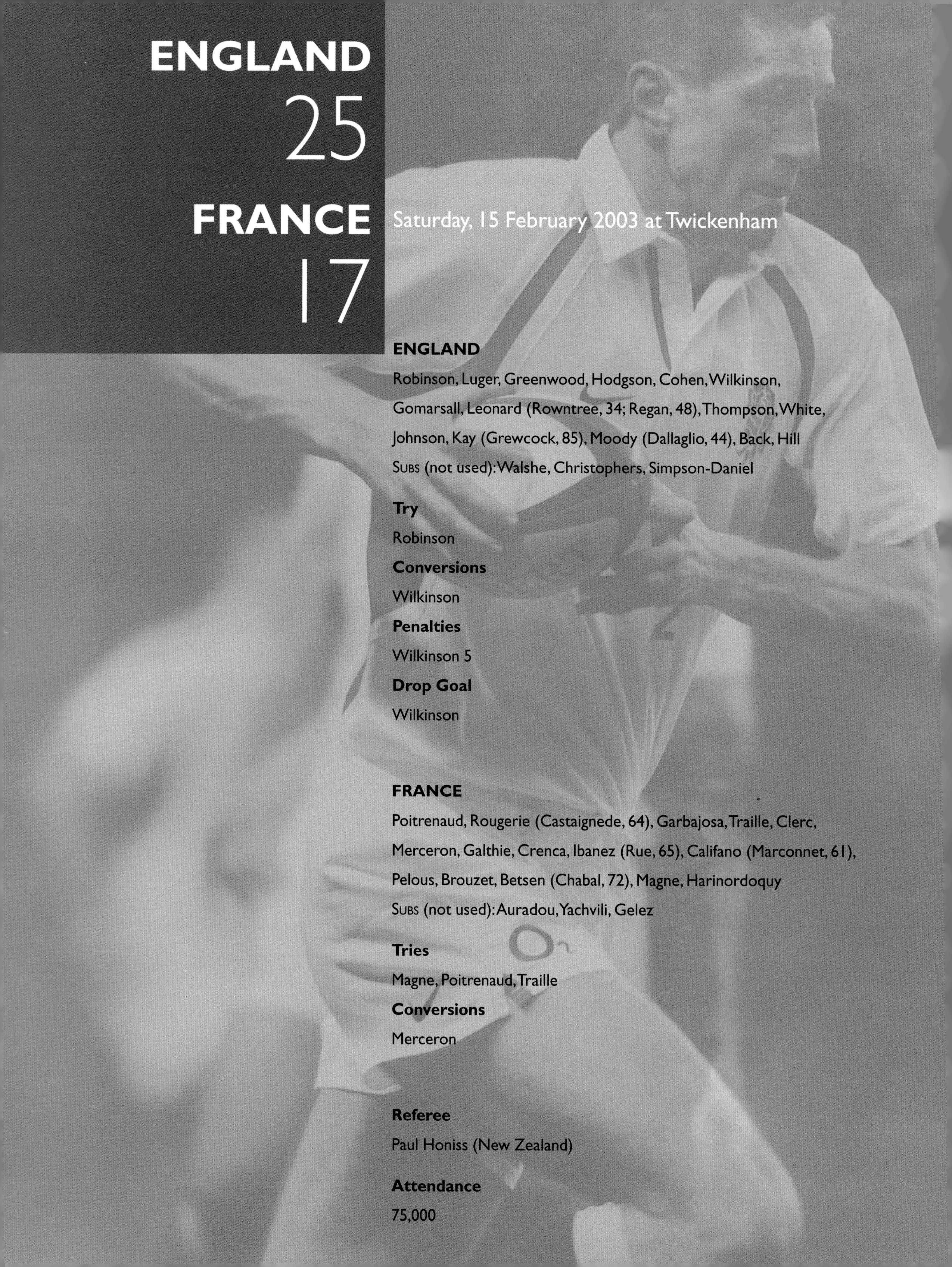

ENGLAND 25

FRANCE 17

Saturday, 15 February 2003 at Twickenham

ENGLAND

Robinson, Luger, Greenwood, Hodgson, Cohen, Wilkinson, Gomarsall, Leonard (Rowntree, 34; Regan, 48), Thompson, White, Johnson, Kay (Grewcock, 85), Moody (Dallaglio, 44), Back, Hill

SUBS (not used): Walshe, Christophers, Simpson-Daniel

Try

Robinson

Conversions

Wilkinson

Penalties

Wilkinson 5

Drop Goal

Wilkinson

FRANCE

Poitrenaud, Rougerie (Castaignede, 64), Garbajosa, Traille, Clerc, Merceron, Galthie, Crenca, Ibanez (Rue, 65), Califano (Marconnet, 61), Pelous, Brouzet, Betsen (Chabal, 72), Magne, Harinordoquy

SUBS (not used): Auradou, Yachvili, Gelez

Tries

Magne, Poitrenaud, Traille

Conversions

Merceron

Referee

Paul Honiss (New Zealand)

Attendance

75,000

'…we'll be taking a close look at our selections over the next few days'

To many, the coming together of the past two Six Nations champions on the first weekend of the 2003 Royal Bank of Scotland Six Nations at Twickenham would, to all intents and purposes, be the deciding fixture of the series. Whoever emerged the victors, so the argument went, would become the year's champions, and quite probably Grand Slam holders to boot, in spite of the fact that both would have to make the trip to Lansdowne Road to face a resurgent Ireland. Both England and France were riding high after autumnal successes against the best the Southern Hemisphere had to offer, and both had their sights set even higher than the Grand Slam, eyeing the World Cup later in the year.

It was a must-win test match for England to avenge defeat in Paris a year before and begin their Grand Slam campaign. And for one player it should have held even greater significance. Jason Leonard, in his thirteenth season of playing for England and with his eyes fixed firmly on a fourth World Cup campaign, would be capturing an astonishing hundredth cap in the game. Typically, though, the prop was phlegmatic. 'It's a nice milestone and I'm sure, when I've retired and I look back on my career, I'll cherish it, but right now it doesn't really matter much to me,' Leonard insisted. 'It means a lot more to my friends and family. To be honest, I was a little embarrassed by all the attention. I'm always happy to accommodate

the media, but there was so much interest in the build-up it wasn't the perfect way to prepare for such an important test match. The point is, in international rugby these days, you don't have any time to sit back and congratulate yourself. If you stand still you go backwards.'

One way or another the props would dominate the early news as the countdown to the Six Nations kick-off began in earnest. England suffered a major blow when they lost tighthead Phil Vickery ten days before the France game to a back injury sustained during Gloucester's Heineken Cup campaign. Told he required surgery, Vickery faced a three-month lay-off, which ruled him out of the whole Six Nations tournament. 'To say I was gutted by this news is an understate-

ment,' Vickery said. 'Things had been going really well for me up until then. My lower back had been sore and I'd had a bulging disc for years, but that goes with the territory when you play in the front row. But for a piece of the disc to get stuck in the nerve was unlucky. I've had to miss quite a few England games over the years through injury, but it doesn't make it any easier when another injury forces you to withdraw, especially when you know you're going to miss out on the whole of the Six Nations.'

Barely twenty-four hours had passed when France, too, lost an influential prop, but for very different reasons. Pieter de Villiers, a French-naturalised South African who had become a permanent fixture in Les Bleus, was suspended by the French Rugby Football Union after testing positive for ecstasy and cocaine. The tighthead faced a possible two-year ban under International Board rules after the random drug test in the previous December. A distraught de Villiers protested his innocence, citing a night out in Paris with his Stade Français teammates as the only possible time when someone might have spiked his drink. 'I am devastated because I cannot understand this,' he said. 'I don't know how these traces got into my body. Some of the team went into Paris after the Harlequins match. I can swear I never consciously took anything that night. Someone could have put something in my beer. It can be the only explanation. I have had many random drug tests with my club and the national French team, but have never tested positive. I am really sorry for my French teammates because this whole affair is giving a bad image to rugby.'

He received some support from a shocked Leonard across the English Channel. 'Pieter's a lovely person,' said the man who would have packed down opposite him in the front row. 'I've been out with him a number of times after games and there's never been anything to make me think he would do anything like that.'

The French coach, Bernard Laporte, was sympathetic towards his prop, but insistent that he could not possibly play against England. 'Pieter is one of the big players of the team but it is important for the spirit of rugby that he does not play at Twickenham next week,' he announced. In Christian Califano, France had a ready-made, world-class replacement.

On the Monday night preceding Saturday's French encounter England Head Coach Clive Woodward announced his team. Fit-again wing Dan Luger was back after an injury had ruled him out of the autumn internationals, and Woodward had kept faith in Lewis Moody,

ABOVE England and France line up for the national anthems on a sombre day for English rugby.

which meant another seat on the bench for Lawrence Dallaglio, but the major surprise came in the centre. Mike Tindall, suffering from an injured shoulder and hip, had skipped training each week in order to turn out for struggling Bath at the weekends. Under such circumstances it was little wonder his form and fitness had deserted him, and no great shock to anyone that Woodward told him he would not be considered for the national team until he regained both. Tindall's replacement, however, was utterly unpredicted. Charlie Hodgson, hitherto Jonny Wilkinson's understudy at stand-off, would make his first Six Nations start. It was another of Woodward's interesting calls,

although his reasoning made sense. The England Head Coach recalled Hodgson's mature display at fly-half in Buenos Aires the summer before, when he helped orchestrate a famous victory over the Pumas. And still fresh in the memory was the job Serge Betsen had done on Wilkinson the previous spring, when the French flanker had virtually hounded the stand-off out of the game. 'France played outstandingly well against Wilkinson and we didn't help ourselves,' Woodward explained. 'We won't be caught again this time. We will be a lot better prepared. Hodgson had a fantastic game in Argentina. He's a great player who will give us clear options which we haven't had in recent games. Wilkinson is the main man. He is the number-one fly-half in the world. I don't want to shift him from that position and I won't be doing that. What we've done isn't rocket science. We have to attack this French team in every facet of the game. They believe they are stronger at scrum and line-out so it will be an interesting day all round.'

Hodgson received the news on his mobile phone at a motorway service station on the Sunday night en route from Manchester to London. 'Jonny will call all the shots and I'm there to help him, to be on the lookout for him as an extra pair of eyes,' the Sale Shark said in reaction to the news. 'It will definitely help Jonny out and put some doubt

ABOVE Charlie Hodgson, here in pursuit of Xavier Garbajosa, made his first Six Nations start against France.

RIGHT Jason Robinson proves too fast for Raphael Ibanez.

into French minds. Sometimes I'll be at ten, Jonny at twelve and vice versa.'

Luger was both delighted and surprised to be back so quickly into the England fold. 'I'd played only four games for Harlequins so I wasn't expecting to be back in the squad, let alone make the starting fifteen,' he admitted. 'The wings had done very well during the autumn, so it was a huge boost for me to get straight back in.'

Dallaglio, meanwhile, took his latest setback on the chin. 'I was obviously disappointed and I didn't agree with the selectors decision again, but I also knew that with a tournament consisting of five games in just seven weeks that my chance would come and that I'd have to take it.'

After the selection surprises had been digested, the media turned its focus firmly on to the forthcoming centurion. Confirmation of Leonard's place at loosehead in the starting

fifteen began a few days of national celebration within English rugby. In winning his hundredth cap Leonard, already the most capped forward in the history of the sport, would join just two elite rugby players. The Australian wing, David Campese, had retired on 101 caps, while the current record holder, French centre Philippe Sella, called it a day on 111. Both would concede that playing in the coal face of rugby in the front row was a completely different proposition to what they had endured. Debuting in Argentina back in 1990, the East Ender from Barking had since played in three World Cups, had gone on three British and Irish Lions tours, and had won three Grand Slams. His captain, Martin Johnson, normally not one to eulogise, on this made an exception. 'I don't think anyone will ever reach a hundred caps again in test rugby,' he said. 'The game is too physical nowadays, and players are receiving too many injuries and knocks. To achieve one hundred caps in any position is extraordinary. To achieve it as a prop is nothing short of phenomenal. Not only that, but Jason has learned to adapt to the many changes in the game since he started out. He's playing better than ever.'

The day after England's selection news, France announced their team for Twickenham. As expected, Califano, revitalised since joining Saracens, filled the gap left by de Villiers. Xavier Garbajosa was preferred to Thomas Castaignede in the centre spot absented by the influential New Zealand-born centre Tony Marsh, who would miss the tournament following knee surgery. With the likes of their inspirational captain Fabien Galthie, Damian Traille and the new find of French rugby, wing Vincent Clerc, France once again posed a serious threat to England's stunning unbeaten home record and to their Grand Slam hopes. As usual, however, everything depended on which French team would be showing up at Twickenham. As Galthie succinctly put it: 'We can soar with the eagles or we can be terrible.'

Serge Betsen, the French flanker born in the Cameroon but raised in Paris, took time out to talk of Wilkinson, the man he managed to ensnare twelve months earlier. This time, he reasoned, it would not be so easy. 'Wilkinson is like the genie,' he explained. 'Let him out of the bottle and you will be in trouble. He can do everything and do it all quickly. Two metres away from the defence he can kick, pass or take the gap. It needed a collective effort to look after him in Paris last year but this will be much more difficult. England have a frightening record at Twickenham and Wilkinson is the best. Every day this week I have watched him on video.'

Meanwhile, team manager Jo Maso was spicing up the

game with historical rhetoric. 'The French and English people don't like each other,' he proclaimed. 'It's a lasting fact since the Hundred Years War, since Joan of Arc. Our sport allows people to fight on the pitch the wars they cannot fight any more on the battlefield.'

Twenty-four hours before the start of the 2003 Six Nations England were dealt a blow with the news that scrum-half Matt Dawson was dropping out of the team, having failed to recover from a calf injury. Gloucester's Andy Gomarsall would fill the gap, starting a championship game for the first time since losing at home to France six years before. That defeat saw Gomarsall, then at Wasps, lose his place to Austin Healey. It took him five long years to win it back, when he played his part in the win in Argentina in

2002. Nick Walshe, Sale's uncapped scrum-half, would be reserve, as Kyran Bracken was recovering from concussion and Healey out of the whole tournament with an Achilles-tendon condition. 'I'd gone home for the rest day on the Thursday and was in the process of renting out a video when I received a call from a local journalist congratulating me,' Gomarsall recalled. 'I asked him for what. Then I noticed I'd had a missed call and it was Clive Woodward's number. Clive was brilliant. He stressed how well I'd been playing for Gloucester, and what a good job I did against Argentina and when I came on against South Africa, so he had no worries about me at all. That put me at ease, and the fact that I'd been training all week with the team in any case meant that the step up would be relatively seamless.'

ABOVE It takes two to tackle Cohen.

Neil Back was in a positive mood as the start of the Six Nations loomed. 'I'm putting my neck on the line here by stating right now that England will not only win the tournament, but the Grand Slam as well,' he said. 'Why? Because this has to be the year when we finally pull it off. As for France, they caught us cold last time, and we didn't provide the help Jonny Wilkinson needed. It will be different this time.'

It was left to Martin Johnson to remind an expectant English rugby public that beating France a day later would be no mean feat. 'Anticipation for this game has been building ever since both sides finished a successful autumn series against the big three Southern Hemisphere countries,' Johnson said. 'I'm expecting it to be tough and to go down to the wire because there's very little between us. We're the favourites, but only because we're playing at Twickenham. That, I hope, will give us the edge. But

ABOVE It takes two to tackle Cohen.

nobody should bet too much money on either of us. It's going to be too close for that.'

That should have been that. The night before an England test match should be a time for reflection and nerves, for last-minute preparations and no distractions. Instead, the England squad was presented with devastating news. Nick Duncombe, the popular England and Harlequins scrum-half, had died in Lanzarote while warm-weather training and recuperating from injury. The twenty-one-year-old, who had won two caps for England the previous year, thereby becoming his country's youngest ever scrum-half, died from a rare bacterial infection. Doctors would later disclose that his death had been caused by cardiac and respiratory failure due to sepsis.

Mark Evans, the Harlequins chief executive, arrived at the England team hotel in Bagshot on the Friday night to break the news. He took it upon himself personally to relate Duncombe's death to the three Quins players in the England starting fifteen: Jason Leonard, whose centenary celebrations suddenly became inconsequential; Will Greenwood, who had suffered terribly after the loss of his baby boy just five months previously; and Dan Luger, a particularly close friend of Nick. Clive Woodward then assembled the whole team to reveal the tragedy. Nothing was said publicly about Duncombe by the England party until the Saturday evening, after the France game was over, but the sombre news must have made performing against such world-class opposition much more difficult, as well as trivialising the result to a large extent.

By late Saturday morning, the news had filtered out. Wearing an armband on his tracksuit sleeve, a dejected-looking Jason Leonard was handed the honour of running out alone on to the Twickenham pitch to receive a standing ovation from the sell-out crowd in honour of his century of caps. Johnson led out the rest of the team shortly afterwards, all sporting black armbands. A perfectly observed minute's silence followed in memory of Duncombe, the England team linking arms and bowing heads before having to focus all their attention on the small matter of defeating the reigning Six Nations champions. It had been one of the most emotional moments ever witnessed at headquarters. Now it was time to play test-match rugby.

Against a good-looking French team, a combination of man-of-the-match Jonny Wilkinson's impeccable kicking and some individual brilliance from Jason Robinson won the day, but a late flourish from France made the final few minutes unnecessarily tense for England. Indeed, the visitors outscored England by three tries to one and, if Gerald Merceron or Damien Traille had converted four missed penalty and conversion chances, the French would have won. In contrast, Wilkinson made the most of all five of his penalty chances, as well as adding a drop goal. His unerring accuracy secured England their nineteenth straight win at Fortress Twickenham.

The manner in which England, through Wilkinson, took a 14th-minute lead was unusually fortunate. Faced with a tricky kick into the teeth of a blustery wind, the Newcastle stand-off watched as the ball bounced off the crossbar and over for three points. 'I'd been working on those rebounds-off-the-crossbar kicks,' Wilkinson would say later with a wry smile. In what was always going to be a tight affair, every point would count and the early lead appeared crucial.

France, though, hit back immediately. As befitting a team who looked to be on a World Cup semi-final collision course with England in the following autumn, they exploited centre Charlie Hodgson's inexperience in his new position.. The Sale stand-off had never played at centre at any level of senior rugby, but in the 16th minute he was faced with a typical centre's problem – having to clear from inside his own twenty-two in the face of on-rushing opposition flankers. Olivier Magne charged down the punt, caught the ball on the bounce and dived over close enough to the posts to make Merceron's conversion a formality.

'My first reaction as I saw Magne score was, "Oh no, what have I done?"' Hodgson said. 'As I stood under the posts waiting for the conversion I knew the boys wouldn't give me stick for it, but I needed a minute or two to clear my head. I was still annoyed with myself when Jonny Wilkinson was taking a penalty shortly afterwards, but Neil Back came up to me and said, "Forget it, what's done is done. It's time to move on." After that I felt a lot better.'

England resorted to their grinding best, knowing that in Wilkinson they possess a man with a left foot that can break any team's heart. Three of his penalties, two stemming from poor discipline by prop Jean-Jacques Crenca, handed England a useful 12–7 lead at the break.

By then, Leonard had limped off the field to his second standing ovation of the afternoon. Ironically, in his hundredth international, the affable prop had pulled a hamstring for the first time in his career. Despite the tension of the game, and the trauma of Nick Duncombe's death, it provoked a moment of mirth for Woodward, who, seeing Leonard's incredulous expression when told of his pulled muscle, burst out laughing. Leonard explained, 'I was absolutely gobsmacked when I discovered what I'd done. The only saving grace from my point of view is that I'm glad to say I didn't do it running. I was trying to rip the ball out of a French forward's hands and was bent over, placing much of my weight and balance on my hamstring. During this manoeuvre another French forward came in and hit me hard, which placed a great deal more pressure on the hamstring, which resulted in the injury.'

Graham Rowntree proved to be a worthy replacement and, unperturbed, England laid siege to the French line early into the second half. At this point, though, Moody's shoulder gave way again. 'After the South Africa game I had a minor operation on the shoulder and honestly felt that everything had been cured after a lot of training had prepared me for the Six

Nations,' he said. 'Then I attempted to charge down a kick and landed smack on the shoulder. This time I knew it was more serious. I didn't think it would put me out of the rest of the season, but I certainly felt it could be the end of my role in the Six Nations.' Indeed it was, and he would not even be fit to take a place on England's summer tour Down Under.

Soon after Moody's exit, though, the moment of the match arrived. In essence a long pass from Will Greenwood set Jason Robinson free to scuttle over in the 48th minute close to the posts. But there was much more to the try than this. Greenwood, by his own admission, is not the world's fastest back, nor necessarily the most fearsome defensively, but when it comes to vision there is no better player in the world game. Seeing what is on, deciding what action to take and then executing a move in a split second is Greenwood's forte.

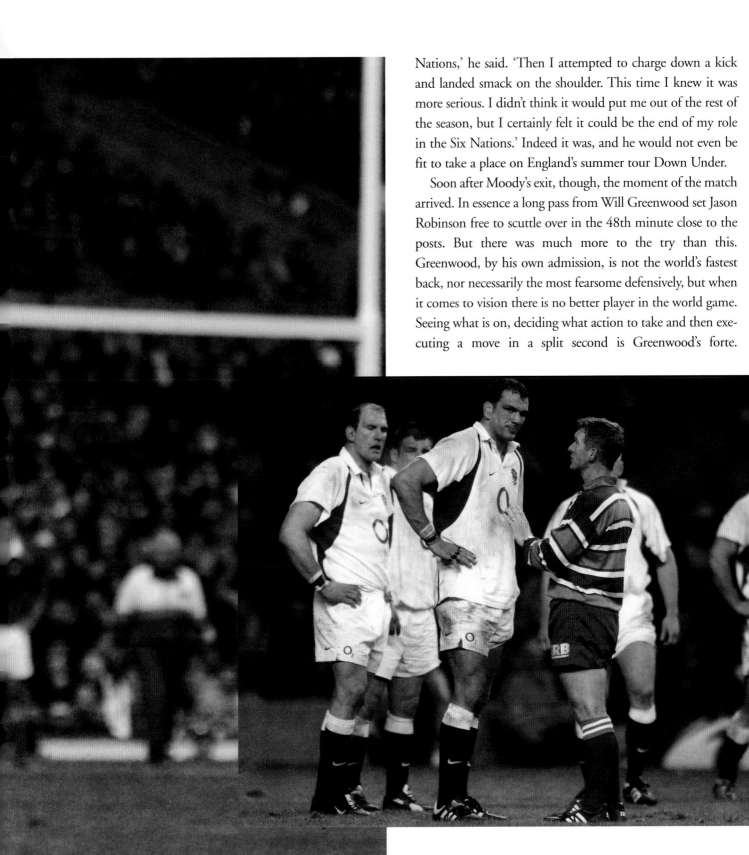

ABOVE Referee Paul Honiss explains himself to Martin Johnson.

LEFT The hardest angle for a left-footer made easy by Wilkinson.

Although Robinson's name is next to the try, his ninth in fifteen tests, he would not have been able to score without Greenwood's lofted pass, so perfectly weighted that it left Aurelien Rougerie stranded as the English full-back's sudden burst of speed took him through the final remnants of the French defence.

Robinson, of course, still had to produce a scintillating run from full-back and arrive for the pass at speed. A shade disappointing in the autumn internationals, but only because the Southern Hemisphere teams had him well marshalled, Robinson was back to his snapping, jinking best against France. 'You know that if you put the ball invitingly in front of Jason ten yards from the line he won't miss,' said Greenwood afterwards. 'It was almost rugby league style in execution, which of course would have made it familiar to Jason. The delay in the pass and the fact that one of the their players had jumped out of their defensive line meant that there was no one in front of Jason.'

The try pulled England clear at 19–7, a big enough lead to start dispelling any fears of another French victory and Grand Slam gone begging. It was also the highlight from a team which failed to produce its usual all-singing, all-dancing performance. In truth, only a thirty-minute spell of rugby was top drawer from England on the day, but it would prove to be enough.

Wilkinson slotted home his fifth penalty of the afternoon, a routine score if it had not been for the milestone the three points achieved. In successfully converting his chance, Wilkinson passed 600 test-match points in only his thirty-ninth international. In doing so he reached such a mark quicker than any player in the history of the game, and now stood below an elite band consisting of Grant Fox, Hugo Porta, Gavin Hastings, Matt Burke, Andrew Mehrtens, Michael Lynagh, Diego Dominguez and Neil Jenkins, whose world record of 1,091 points looks under serious threat from the voraciously hungry Wilkinson. Moreover, he could not have turned the tables on his tormentor from a year before more convincingly. This time there was no repeat of the mauling handed out by French flanker Serge Betsen. Twelve months earlier Wilkinson had been forced to leave the fray early. Now it was Betsen's turn, removed with eighteen minutes remaining. As if to drive home his point, Wilkinson then struck over a sweet drop goal from thirty metres out to ease England into a 25–7 lead, seemingly out of reach and out of sight.

'The year before France prepared specifically for us, did their homework well, and came up with the performance on the day,' Wilkinson explained. 'They defended as if there were double the amount of players in their side, and they made life very hard for myself. But we've moved on since then. This time our back row were much more proactive and productive. We were able to stamp our authority and not worry about having to deal with what the French back row threw at us.'

France, though, were not quite finished. They scored their second try when Thomas Castaignede, just off the bench for Rougerie, was involved in a sweeping backs' move that saw full-back Clement Poitrenaud score in the corner, although it took video referee Jim Fleming to confirm the points.

To the England management's discomfort, France then scored again when the centre, Traille, plunged over in the corner in injury time. However, his missed conversion left France still eight points in arrears as time ran out.

The celebrations on the field were muted. England had cleared a very tricky first hurdle, they had avenged the previous season's defeat in Paris, and the dream of a Grand Slam remained intact, but in the Twickenham gloom such feats could not have been further from the thoughts of the England players. It was only an hour later, once the management and players had showered and changed into their suits in readiness for the usual post-match dinner, that the full impact of Nick Duncombe's death on the team was revealed. 'The stupid thing is if Nick had not been injured, with Matt Dawson already out, he may well have been on the bench today against France,' revealed Woodward. 'It's absolutely tragic but we had

to pull ourselves together quickly and get on with it. I'm sure Nick would have been proud of the way we played out there. It's been a very difficult couple of days for us and I'd like to pay particular tribute to the way the Quins players performed. I know they are all in bits over Nick's death.'

Indeed, they were. Phil Larder admitted that the management had to give serious consideration to withdrawing an emotional Dan Luger from the team. 'We had a word with Dan and tears were welling in his eyes,' said Larder. 'He was so upset that we asked him if he could handle it. He said he could, that Nick would have wanted him to play and help make sure that we beat France.'

Luger himself had considered pulling out and he was too upset to attend the post-match dinner. 'It took a great effort of will to get up after a sleepless night and prepare,' he said. 'Every time the ball came near me I half imagined that Nick was floating one of his wonderful passes into my hands. I had a few tears during the National Anthem. I can't believe he's dead. I played in a daze. I've never felt like this on a rugby field before. Nick was the toughest of the tough.'

The eloquent Will Greenwood was similarly affected. 'It was very difficult to deal with but, standing there, you asked yourself a few questions. Would Nick have wanted you to crawl away, curl into a ball and not turn up? That wasn't the kind of kid he was. You don't come back from a broken neck as he did to play for England without being a real fighter. He was such a nice kid. Nobody deserves that at twenty-one years of age.'

Perhaps the most fitting tribute, however, came from a clearly distressed Jason Leonard, who received a gold cap to mark his century at the dinner. 'A star that flickers twice as bright, like Nick Duncombe, flickers only half as long,' he said. 'Nick's been in my thoughts from the moment we heard the news. Even during the game I couldn't help thinking of him. I'd only received a text message from him out in Lanzarote three days earlier. Not many of the team would have slept well the night before, I can assure you. All the players are choked. There's a real sense of shock. The trick was to try to keep busy because otherwise you would think. The worst time was on the bus journey from the team hotel to Twickenham. Then it's always quiet, and that's when I thought of Nick constantly. My hundredth cap meant a lot to me but today was about making a good start to an important year and a tribute to Nick.'

When Clive Woodward could finally bring himself to talk about the importance of the victory over France his message

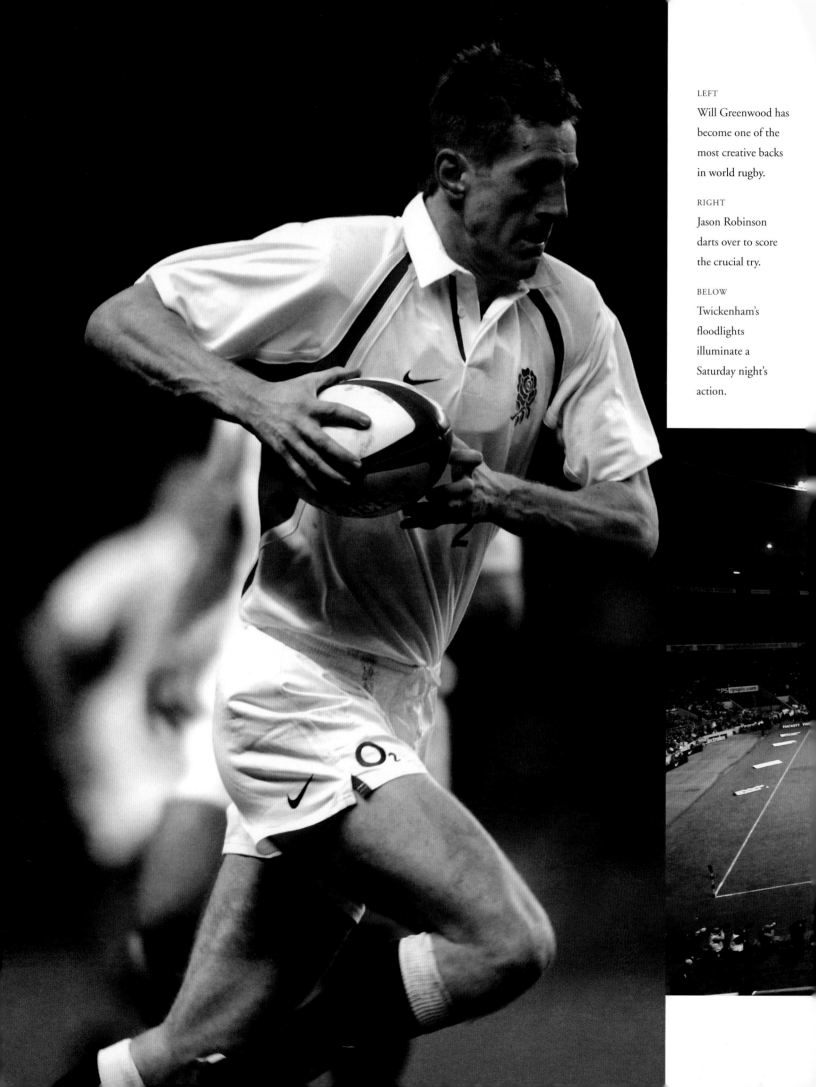

LEFT
Will Greenwood has become one of the most creative backs in world rugby.

RIGHT
Jason Robinson darts over to score the crucial try.

BELOW
Twickenham's floodlights illuminate a Saturday night's action.

was stark. 'The ramifications of losing today couldn't bear thinking of,' the England Head Coach claimed. 'It was a complete must-win match for us. I can't overstate the importance of this win, not only in a Six Nations context, but also looking at the wider picture and the World Cup. That said, the last twenty-five minutes were the worst England have played in a long time, and we'll be taking a close look at our selections over the next few days.'

There was little time to spare. One week later England would be facing Wales at the imposing Millennium Stadium, which meant it would be straight back down to business for Woodward and his men. There was no opportunity to celebrate the win over France, but, then again, there was no inclination to either. The team had to recover from Nick Duncombe's death quickly, and recover they would, but the young scrum-half would never be forgotten.

WALES
9

ENGLAND
26

Saturday, 22 February 2003 at the Millennium Stadium, Cardi

WALES

K. Morgan, R. Williams (Harris, 66), Taylor, Shanklin (Watkins, 64),
G. Thomas (Charvis, 67), Sweeney, G. Cooper, I. Thomas, Humphreys
(G. Williams, 67), Evans (Jenkins, 67), S. Williams (Llewellyn, 73), Sidoli,
D. Jones, M. Williams, G. Thomas

SUB (not used): Peel

Penalties

Sweeney 3

ENGLAND

Robinson (Christophers, 38), Luger, Greenwood, Hodgson,
Cohen (Gomarsall, 80), Wilkinson (Simpson-Daniel, 78), Bracken,
Rowntree, Thompson, Morris, Johnson, Kay (Grewcock, 62),
Hill (Simpson-Daniel, 41–51), Back (J. Worsley, 55), Dallaglio.

SUBS (not used): Regan, M. Worsley

Tries

Greenwood, J. Worsley

Conversions

Wilkinson 2

Penalties

Wilkinson 2

Drop Goal

Wilkinson 2

Referee

S. Walsh (New Zealand)

Attendance

72,500

'Being overwhelming favourites puts us in quite a dangerous position'

The weight of expectation on England's sorrowful shoulders was heavy after the first weekend's action in the Six Nations tournament. While England were seeing off France at Twickenham, Wales were going down in Rome by 30–22 to a much-improved Italian side under the new guidance of former All Black great John Kirwan. If the Italians were better than many expected, though, Wales certainly contributed to their own demise. Welsh rugby had been riddled with internal fighting surrounding the future of their clubs and the efforts of their new chief executive, David Moffett, to introduce provincial rugby. Losing, and deservedly so, to Italy was a new low for Welsh rugby, though.

All England had to do, so the pundits argued, was turn up in Cardiff and the win was theirs. This was reflected in the absurd odds of 1–25 on an England win offered by the bookmakers. Anyone who had actually faced the Welsh at the Millennium Stadium would explain that it is never as simple as that. Anyone who had faced the Welsh in an England jersey could verify that the chance to put one over the unloved English always resulted in a significant raising of the Celtic game.

The England team named by Clive Woodward on the Monday evening, forty-eight hours after the win over France, included some changes enforced by injury, plus one notable shake-up in the half-back department. The pack that finished the job against France would be beginning the next challenge in Cardiff, which meant Graham Rowntree replacing a ham-

Throughout that time he had battled against the likes of Austin Healey, Gomarsall and, in particular, Matt Dawson. The friendly rivalry between Bracken and Dawson has meant that, over a period of eight years, neither has worn the number-nine jersey for more than a season at a time, with Dawson's run of eight consecutive matches in the late nineties being the recent record at scrum-half. Thirty-one-year-old Bracken's future England prospects had not looked too clever when he was omitted from the squad for the autumn Southern Hemisphere series, and when Dawson had dropped out of the squad to face France the previous week Bracken was still recovering from concussion. Having just been cleared by a neurosurgeon to resume playing following a precautionary brain scan, he received the news of his recall at home on the Monday night.

LEFT Old and new: Neil Back supports new boy Robbie Morris on the scrum machine.

RIGHT Jonny Wilkinson scores again.

string-hampered Leonard, who now faced a race to play any part in the remaining Six Nations matches. The young, uncapped London Irish prop Mike Worsley was promoted to the bench for the first time. Lewis Moody was out too, of course, which meant Lawrence Dallaglio would be starting alongside his two old back-row allies, Richard Hill and Neil Back.

The big surprise was that scrum-half Kyran Bracken was recalled at scrum-half in place of Andy Gomarsall, who had failed to take his chance against the French. This was the twelfth time a surprised Bracken had been recalled to the England team during his ten-year international career.

'To be honest, I was hoping I might get another chance, whether that was because someone had lost form or got injured,' the Saracens player confided. 'I didn't think the chance would come this week, though. I've been in the squad for ten years now and every year has been a battle. But it's tough at the top and when you've got it, you've got to hold on to it.'

'Had Matt been fit he would have played,' conceded Woodward. 'Kyran just gets the nod, which is very tough on Andy Gomarsall, but his club form has not been what it was before Christmas.'

Dan Luger kept his place on the wing, despite stiff challenges from the likes of James Simpson-Daniel and Phil Christophers. He was still clearly bothered, though, by Nick Duncombe's death throughout the week running up to the game in Cardiff. 'Maybe it will make me stronger,' Luger reflected. 'Maybe it will make me realise certain things about life, that you have to enjoy it while you can. I'm sure this has made everyone question the meaning of life. Even people who didn't know Nick have been hit pretty hard. Making the most of life is easily said, and it all sounds a bit like a cliché, but it's true.

'Part of me would like to go away and grieve properly. This week will be harder than last week because it's sunk in now. I'm having to hold it in. I've never experienced anything like this before and maybe it's easier being kept occupied and being around people who mean a lot to me.'

The following day another change was necessary in the English front row. Robbie Morris, who had won a silver medal at the junior Commonwealth Games three years earlier, was called into the team as the fourth-choice tighthead. Morris, at twenty-one still seen as a novice at his club, Northampton, let alone for England, had been plucked straight out of the previous week's England A team against the French to replace Julian White, who had broken down in training. Surgery on White's knee the next day would keep him out of action for six weeks. As the sick-list already included props Phil Vickery and Jason Leonard, Morris suddenly found himself catapulted into the big league. A debut at the Millennium Stadium would be quite a way to open his international account.

Wales, meanwhile, deliberately delayed the naming of their team by a day. They had come to the conclusion that they had named their team too early prior to losing in Rome. 'We want to keep people guessing,' explained Alan Phillips, the Wales manager. 'Last week the players knew the line-up on Monday and that encouraged them to be complacent. We want to keep people on their toes throughout the week and maybe this will help.' Twenty-four hours later the Welsh team was finally posted, and it was a team-sheet so full of surprises that it made Clive Woodward's selections seem positively tame in comparison. Out of the eight changes, the biggest gamble was on the reappointment of Jonathan Humphreys as captain. He had been given the task of bringing some passion back into the team. The Bath hooker, just shy of his thirty-fourth birthday, would be coming back where he had gone out, against the same opponents in the same city. Humphreys lost the captaincy after losing to England in the last match at the old Arms Park in 1997, and had been away from international rugby since the previous World Cup more than three years before. 'This is something I never thought would happen again,' admitted Humphreys. 'It came as a massive shock but I'd never turn it down. I'm over the moon.' His coach, New Zealander Steve Hansen, had demoted former captain Colin Charvis and appointed

Humphreys because he wanted 'leadership'. He was honest enough to admit to the massive risk he was taking, however. 'If it works, I'm a genius,' he said. 'If it does not, then I'm a bloody idiot.'

Charvis was replaced by another Bath player, Gavin Thomas, in the back row and demoted to the bench. Elsewhere, the removal of Iestyn Harris and Dwayne Peel cleared the way for a brand-new half-back pairing of Pontypridd's Ceri Sweeney at stand-off and Gareth Cooper, a third Bath player, at scrum-half. Cooper, for one, was determined not to allow England to walk away with the kind of win the bookmakers expected. 'People are saying they're going to hammer us but that shows little respect,' he said. 'That really gets to me. We need to show them we're not going to lie down, and come out with all guns blazing.'

Although everyone else was expecting a comfortable English win, the England camp was wisely preparing for any-

thing and everything. 'I cannot contemplate driving back over the Severn Bridge without having won this game,' said Clive Woodward on the eve of the match. 'The ramifications of England losing are huge, but that's the pressure of the whole occasion. Wales are in a corner, which makes them extremely dangerous.'

Lawrence Dallaglio, stung as captain by the Welsh at Wembley three years previously, was quick to take up his Head Coach's point. 'Being overwhelming favourites puts us in quite a dangerous position,' he declared. 'We have to respect Wales and we will.'

For a nation expecting doom, the home support inside the Millennium Stadium come Saturday afternoon reached a

LEFT Tom Shanklin upends Will Greenwood.

RIGHT Lawrence Dallaglio wraps his arms around Gareth Cooper.

deafening crescendo shortly after they had completed a mass rendition of Tom Jones's signature song, 'Delilah'. Humphreys, in a shrewd move, had led his side on a number of jogged laps around the stadium, partly to bolster support, and partly to remind his troops how much a win, or at least a passionate performance, would mean to the Welsh. Emerging later from the players' tunnel for the game, the Welsh aped David Sole's famous slow trudge at Murrayfield before Scotland went on to beat England and win the 1990 Grand Slam.

What followed may have been the England victory that the word of rugby had expected, but it was nothing like the contemptuous rout predicted by even the most

fervent of home supporters. Although second-half tries from the magnificent Will Greenwood and Joe Worsley put the game beyond the reach of the opposition, a wonderful rebirth of Welsh passion was witnessed on that Saturday evening in Cardiff. Suggestions that had been made earlier in the week for a future two-tiered Six Nations tournament were thoroughly rubbished. Clive Woodward's team were too professional and polished to buckle under the sometimes intense Welsh pressure but, at the end of the affair, they certainly knew they had been in a battle.

'This game was as tough as those against the Southern Hemisphere sides in the autumn, and I could think of nothing worse than a two-tiered Six Nations,' said the England Head Coach afterwards. 'You won't find anyone in the England camp who would want to go down this line. We achieved our two objectives of winning and not conceding a

try. But the Welsh should be applauded for their part in what proved to be a full-on test match.'

Indeed they should. Wales rediscovered the fight that had been so absent in Rome seven days earlier. Perhaps their vibrant display had much to do with an emergency meeting of the Welsh Rugby Union set for the following day that would create five provinces, ending more than 100 years of club tradition, and see 100-plus Welsh players lose their jobs. Many of the men in red were not just playing a Six Nations game. They were playing for their livelihoods.

Early on, Humphreys cleverly ensured that Wales would slow the game down at every opportunity. The expected fast and furious pace many felt Wales would produce would only play into England's hands, as it had done two years previously at the Millennium Stadium. And when debutant stand-off Ceri Sweeney handed Wales an 8th-minute lead with a penalty, there were those who began to dream the impossible.

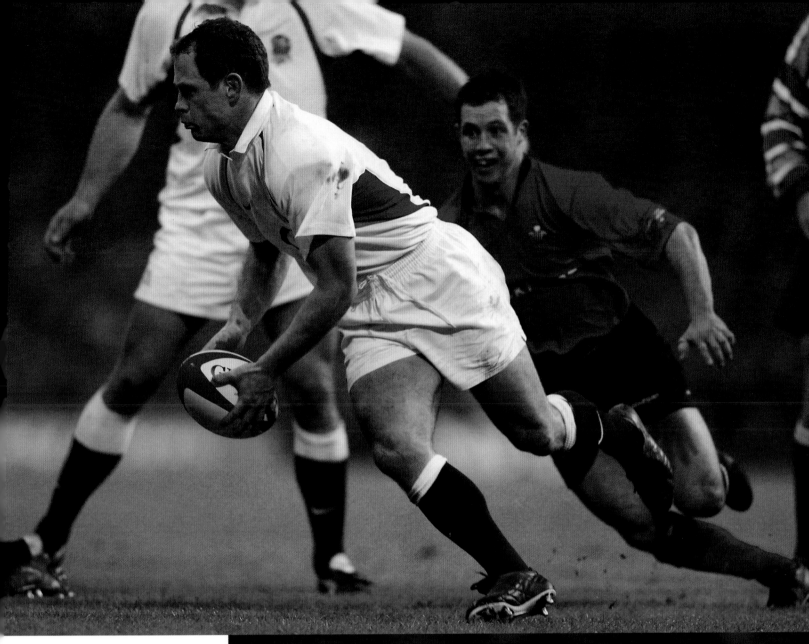

ABOVE Kyran Bracken enjoys his recall to the England team, while Jonny Wilkinson (right) lies injured.

ABOVE LEFT Wilkinson looks to Charlie Hodgson for support.

Although Jonny Wilkinson soon replied with a penalty of his own, the Welsh policy of hustling and harrying England's celebrated stand-off seemed to be working as his team were denied the control they were seeking. A beautifully executed Wilkinson drop goal nudged England ahead, only for Sweeney to level the scores with his second penalty of the evening. A second Wilkinson drop goal handed England a slender half-time lead, but not before two moments of high

Instead, he chose to go for the score himself and was bundled over by the England pair. In the process Robinson twisted his knee and hobbled off the field. 'The boys didn't make it an easy decision for Taylor,' Will Greenwood reflected later. 'They didn't make a decision for him. They call it mug's alley when you're conned into a channel, and although Mark Taylor's a world-class player, he'll think about that chance for quite some time to come. In international rugby you don't get

drama in the dying seconds of the half that proved, ultimately, to be the turning points of the game. First Mark Taylor slipped past Charlie Hodgson's challenge in the centre and sprinted fifty metres towards the England line. To his left were Kevin Morgan and, closer still, Rhys Williams. With Ben Cohen and Jason Robinson standing between him and the line, all Taylor had to do was offload the ball for a certain try.

too many chances and if you don't take them you tend to get beaten. We've learned that ourselves over the past few years.'

Both Cohen and Robinson were already injured before they jointly pulled off the Taylor tackle. 'I'd torn my thigh muscle,' Cohen said. 'I certainly couldn't get up to full pace. But as Taylor came at us Jason's positioning caught him in two minds. He made him think he could score by himself by selling a dummy, but we were ready for this and between us stopped him close to the line. In all honesty, he should have passed and, if he had, Wales would have scored, but it's easier said than done. Certainly it would not have been a good time to have conceded a try from an England point of view. I'm not saying we would have lost the game, but Wales would have gone in at half-time ahead. Their belief would have been sky high and the crowd, who had created an unbelievable atmosphere that night, would have been even noisier.'

The try might indeed have made all the difference in the second half, but, within moments, the Welsh had another chance to score. Phil Christophers replaced Robinson to make his first Six Nations appearance, and was banished from the field within seconds. When Sweeney sent a cross-

moments after I'd come on wasn't exactly in my plans,' a rueful Christophers acknowledged later. 'It was probably *Guinness Book of Records* stuff. I've been told it is a record in international rugby, and not one I'm especially proud of. What happened was that I'd just been on a few seconds and obviously hadn't quite got my bearings when the ball was kicked high across the field towards me. I completely lost the ball in the lights of the stadium roof and ran straight into Thomas. Anyone who knows me as a person and a rugby player knows that I've never fouled anyone in my life, at least not purposefully, but as soon as it happened I knew I'd be off. To be fair, I'd have awarded a yellow card, too.

'As I ran off the pitch I felt dreadful. This was not what I had been dreaming about since the age of four. I felt as if I'd

LEFT The ever-mobile Steve Thompson in familiar guise.

RIGHT An injured Back is helped off the Millennium Stadium pitch.

field chip towards a sprinting Gareth Thomas close to the England line, the Bristol player took out the Welsh wing before Thomas had managed to clasp the ball. Steve Walsh had little choice but to send the England replacement to the sin bin. Christophers had been on the pitch for barely ninety seconds, and had not once touched the ball, when he received his marching orders. 'To be sent to the sin bin

let myself down and, more to the point, I'd let my team down. As the ten minutes passed, though, I became really motivated to make amends when I returned to the pitch. By the time I was back on it was all forgotten.'

He could have no real complaints, and was perhaps fortunate to concede just a penalty. Although this was the correct decision by referee Walsh, penalty tries have been given for less. When Sweeney missed with his penalty kick, Wales returned to the half-time dressing-room still three points in arrears when they could, and should, have been leading. Still, they knew they would have close to ten minutes at the start of the second half with a one-man advantage over England because of Christophers' session in the sin bin. So it must have come as hammer-blow to Welsh hopes when England emerged for the second half and enjoyed their best spell of the match. Perhaps the Welsh should have seen it coming. After all, the third quarter had been England's most productive period against all three of the Southern Hemisphere teams in the autumn and against France the previous week.

England gambled on removing Richard Hill from the pack and sending on James Simpson-Daniel to field a full back line. The tactic would work supremely well. Seven minutes into the second half Greenwood spun and burst through two weary tackles from the Welsh pack to touch down close enough to the posts to make Wilkinson's conversion easy. 'At the time I didn't realise it was a number eight and a second-row forward I had to beat,' Greenwood revealed later. 'In hindsight, I'd have probably given the ball to someone else in fear of my life.'

Although he failed to realise it at the time, Greenwood's try took him to a personal landmark. This was the thirty-year-old's sixth try against the Welsh, which drew him level with Gerald Davies and Rory Underwood in the long history of the fixture. Greenwood had also reached the milestone in just five tests. 'It took my father [Dick Greenwood, former England player and coach] to tell me about equalling the try record against Wales the following morning, and he only found out after reading the newspapers,' Greenwood said. 'It's fantastic to be mentioned in the same breath as Gerald and Rory, but, to be honest, I'll enjoy these kind of feats when I'm fifty-five and have got my feet up. Rugby these days is so fast-moving that you have no time to dwell on anything.'

Within seconds of Christophers' return England struck the crucial blow. Barely a minute had passed after Back had limped off with a calf strain when his replacement, Joe Worsley, took full advantage of a Dallaglio surge to bull-doze over from close range with his first touch of the ball. With Wilkinson's conversion, England now held a dominant fourteen-point lead. This was a particularly special moment for Worsley. Out of action with a torn hamstring for eleven weeks, the Wasps back-row forward had not played for England since having a starring role in their win in Buenos Aires the previous June. Since then he had

missed out on all of the autumn internationals, and was still on his way back when he played against France A the week before. 'I spotted a half-gap and went for it from around five metres out,' he explained. 'The reason why I celebrated so wildly was because I was so pumped up, partly due to the atmosphere, but mainly because I'd been out for so long. Although we didn't play especially well afterwards, the try more or less signified the end of the game in terms of it being a contest. It was a dream way to get back into international rugby.'

From this point onwards England might have expected to have run away with the remainder of the game. However, just as against France the week before, they seemed to ease their collective foot off the gas pedal and Wales, beaten but far from unbowed, launched a spirited fight back. It translated into only three points, though, with Sweeney's third penalty of the night, which was cancelled out by Wilkinson's second penalty with nine minutes remaining.

England had done more than enough to see off a rejuvenated Wales, but it was by no means a convincing performance from Woodward's men. For the second week in a row, questions were asked, but to be less than satisfied with a seventeen-point margin of victory in Cardiff proved just how far England had come. Besides, attractive, flowing rugby during previous Six Nations tournaments had won England many plaudits, but no silverware. All that mattered during this campaign was five straight wins, no matter how they were achieved.

On the plus side, Will Greenwood outlined once again his importance to the England cause. His Head Coach was unequivocal: 'Will was outstanding all round,' said Woodward. 'I thought he was brilliant, absolutely world class out there against Wales.' Lawrence Dallaglio, back in the starting fifteen only because of Moody's injury, took his chance with aplomb and took an authoritative role in the thick of the action to produce his best performance in a white jersey for eighteen months. Robbie Morris made an encouraging start to an international career that will surely produce many more caps. Sought out by a Welsh pack expecting this to be England's weak link, the young Northampton prop coped admirably with the pressure. 'A lot of questions were asked of Robbie on his debut and he came forward with the answers,' said assistant coach Andy Robinson.

Less successful was persisting with Charlie Hodgson at inside centre. A supreme stand-off, with quick feet and an ability to make breaks, Hodgson's defence needed work. 'It's been a risk worth taking,' declared Woodward afterwards.

ABOVE Ben Cohen is well marshalled by Wales.

'But it's not the final solution. Nevertheless, the team will have no issues should Hodgson take the field for whatever reason.'

Will Greenwood, for one, had not been in the least surprised by the Welsh effort. 'Wales got among us, smacked us about, knocked us over and to come through all that required cool heads,' he said. 'We are not here to entertain, though. We are here to win test matches and that was one huge physical confrontation.' Both Head Coach Woodward and captain Johnson made visits to the Welsh dressing-room after the match to congratulate their beaten foes. 'Well done' was the message, Johnson reported later. 'Terrific match. They disrupted well, tackled well and had a go at everything. They put us under a lot of pressure. When Mark Taylor made that break and we stopped him from scoring, it was a big moment. Also when we lost Phil Christophers to the sin bin, we coped really well and to score a try with only fourteen men was the turning point for us.'

The Welsh found solace in their performance. 'The political in-fighting has seen us spiralling downwards,' coach Steve Hansen insisted. 'It's hard enough fighting other countries, let alone yourselves. We're doing so much damage to each other. At least we saw some pride back in our game.'

Captain Jonathan Humphreys, who had had to leave the fray fifteen minutes from time with an injury, concurred. 'We wanted to show we had a bit of guts and a bit of passion and the self-belief that we could actually win the game,' he said. 'At half-time we were in with a shout.'

At full-time, however, they had lost. Wales may have won the sympathy vote but England returned home with a second win in the Six Nations. Now Italy and Scotland at Twickenham stood between the team and an increasingly likely Grand Slam decider in Dublin against Ireland. Nobody within the England camp could afford to look any further than Italy in a fortnight's time, however. Two wins were exactly what had been ordered by Woodward and his management team, but England were far from satisfied and were keen to iron out the problems before taking the field at headquarters.

ENGLAND 40

ITALY 5

Sunday, 9 March 2003 at Twickenham

ENGLAND

Lewsey (Bracken, 71), Simpson-Daniel, Greenwood, Tindall, Luger, Wilkinson (Hodgson, 47; Smith, 53), Dawson, Rowntree (M. Worsley, 60), Thompson (Regan, 65), Morris, Grewcock, Kay (Shaw, 58), J. Worsley, Hill (Sanderson, 65), Dallaglio

Tries

Lewsey 2, Thompson, Simpson-Daniel, Tindall, Luger

Conversions

Wilkinson 4, Dawson

ITALY

Mirco Bergamasco, Mazzucato, Vaccari (Peens, 65), Raineri, Dallan (Masi ,17), Pez, Troncon (Mazzantini, 69), De Carli (Castrogiovanni, 49), Festuccia (Ongaro, 74), Martinez, Bezzi, Giacheri (Bortolami, 47), De Rossi, Persico, Phillips (Palmer, 72)

Try

Mirco Bergamasco

Referee

Alain Rolland (Ireland)

Attendance

75,000

CHAPTER SIX

'This is a huge honour for Jonny … I know it's a challenge he will relish'

T he England team that would face a rejuvenated Italy had a very different look to it. Four of the six changes were enforced by injury, but the others came as a result of Clive Woodward's consistent policy of picking form players and not shirking from dropping even those with the biggest of reputations if they were playing below par.

The first of several surprises was the promotion of Jonny Wilkinson to captain in the absence of the injured Martin Johnson. The Leicester lock was fit enough to play in this fixture, but Woodward felt he could afford to let him rest his troublesome Achilles in preparation for the sterner tests to come against Scotland and Ireland.

ABOVE Captain Jonny: Wilkinson in practice before leading England for the first time.

The remarkable Wilkinson story therefore gained another chapter. With Phil Vickery out of the whole tournament, the stand-off had been England's sole vice-captain. In that sense, once Johnson had been removed from the team, Wilkinson's elevation was likely, but it was still an incredible achievement for a man of only twenty-three years of age. He was the youngest England captain since Will Carling had taken the reins fifteen years previously. But Wilkinson had always been precocious: at eighteen he made his international debut; at twenty he took over goal-kicking duties; at twenty-one he had already accumulated 400 international points; and at twenty-two he became the Premiership's youngest captain. 'This is a huge honour for Jonny,' Clive Woodward said. 'I know it's a challenge he will relish.' But he also underlined how this appointment would be a one-off, at least for the time being. 'Martin Johnson will captain the team against Scotland,' he added. 'He was outstanding against France and Wales and I would expect his minor injury not to prevent him playing in a fortnight's time.'

This did not dilute Wilkinson's sense of achievement, however. 'It's not something I ever expected but I am ecstatic that Clive has given me this opportunity,' he said, officially. 'The responsibility is huge, but I'll be preparing as I normally do.' Later, Wilkinson gave a more personal response. 'I had no idea Johnno was even injured,' he revealed. 'When I arrived at the team hotel I thought it would be like every other week. Then Clive summoned me to tell me the news. I felt very privileged, but also instantly anxious as well. I was keen to get on with the first training session because I wanted to see whether the players would respond and take to me as their captain. As it turned out, everyone gave me their total time and dedication right from the outset. It was a huge weight off my shoulders and I realised from early on that I had nothing to worry about.'

Lawrence Dallaglio, back to top form after his demotion during the autumn internationals and the beginning of the Six Nations, would become the new vice-captain in place of Wilkinson. For Dallaglio, England captain until Johnson took over back in 1999, the news followed his successful comeback to the starting line-up against Wales, which had clearly impressed Woodward. 'It hurt Lawrence tremendously but I cannot praise him enough for the way he handled it,' he said. 'No toys were thrown out of the pram. Instead, he gave the team unflinching support.' Dallaglio was understandably pleased, but also cautious as he prepared to face a country he could have registered with due to his Italian-born father. 'Now is not the time to sit back and reflect, but to make sure I have even more of an influence,' he said. 'I've been fortunate in that I've had my chances as a result of injury to others. That said, it just goes to show how you should never be too disheartened, because one minute I'm on the bench, the next I'm England's vice-captain. Your lot can change very quickly in international rugby.'

Jason Robinson's failure to recover from his damaged knee meant a recall for the versatile Wasps back Josh Lewsey, who would play at full-back. This would be Lewsey's seventh cap, but his first at Twickenham, which meant a lot. He revealed that every so often in the middle of the night he would drive down to Twickenham to work out in the gym. 'An empty stadium is haunting,' he said. 'Every time I've been there when everyone else is in bed I realise how much unfinished business there is for me. It's a special feeling being there by yourself, consumed by the enormity of the stadium and with your ambition.' His selection for the following Saturday was vindication for a life-changing decision made eighteen months before that saw him leave the army to concentrate on rugby full time. 'It was a very difficult choice to make, but it came down to one thing,' the twenty-six-year-old explained. 'I had, as I said, unfinished business on the rugby field.' The last time he had turned out for England, against the United States in June 2001, he had done so as Second-Lieutenant Lewsey, Royal Artillery, having swapped life as a rugby professional for Sandhurst. Two months after returning home from the North American tour, however, he realised he could not do justice to both jobs. 'At the time I was hoping to join the 7th Para, Royal Horse Artillery,' he said. 'I know I would have thoroughly enjoyed it, but my rugby insurance would not have covered me to do it.

'The only role that would have been open to me in the army would have been that of a token soldier. I dismissed that idea as disrespectful to my friends. A lot of them are off to the Gulf. Leaving the army was a big decision but, unfortunately, I could no longer combine both roles. In the end I came to the conclusion that if I couldn't do the job properly, I didn't want to do it at all. I talked to my closest friends and they all said how lucky I was to be a professional rugby player, that not everyone gets paid for doing something they love. I'd always made it clear to the army that rugby was my priority.'

His home debut had been a long time coming. Since making his debut in Dunedin five years before on England's infamous 'Tour of Hell', Lewsey had picked up caps in Auckland, Cape Town, Toronto, Vancouver and San Francisco but, with Jason Robinson out, this was his chance. 'Jason shook my hand and said, "Well done, pal." He's always been very positive towards me. Whenever I've been at the England sessions and I've needed to talk to him about any aspect of the full-back role he has always been very helpful. I'm just going to go out now and play my own game.'

Clive Woodward had no qualms about selecting Lewsey. 'International rugby is a very serious matter and we need players one hundred per cent fit,' he explained. 'If anyone is in any doubt, he doesn't play. The medical advice on Jason was that he would not have been fit until Friday or Saturday. It was a no-brainer. Josh has a terrific attitude. He has never allowed the disappointments of my not picking him to affect him. He's a very focused young man who still thinks he's the best full-back in the world.'

James Simpson-Daniel was picked ahead of Phil Christophers to replace the injured Ben Cohen. Danny Grewcock would deputise for Martin Johnson in the second row. And Joe Worsley would fill the back-row vacancy created by Neil Back's injury. The form changes were Matt Dawson reclaiming his place from Kyran Bracken, and Mike Tindall reappearing in place of Charlie Hodgson, who was on the bench to cover for Wilkinson as fly-half and goal-kicker.

Dawson, who has had his fair share of ups and downs in an England jersey, was relieved to be back. 'Every time you don't play for England due to injury or being dropped it dawns on you that you might have played your last international game, so it was enormously pleasing to get straight back into the team once I'd fully recovered from injury,' he

ABOVE A proud day: Wilkinson in charge versus Italy.

said. 'I knew I was in with a shout, but it was still a great thrill to get the nod and I was determined to make sure I kept hold of the position.'

The return of Tindall ended a worrying period for the bulky Bath centre. Dropped for the first two Six Nations games due to poor form and a lack of fitness brought on by a series of niggling injuries, Tindall had taken off to New York for a long weekend with club colleague Ollie Barkley to get away from rugby for a while. He missed the French win in the process, but the break seemed to do him the power of good. 'I wouldn't have selected myself for England,' he admitted. 'When you play for England you have to be completely honest with yourself. Of course, I was disappointed when Clive phoned me to say I wasn't going to be considered until I was back to my best form, but it would have been a lot worse for me if I had played badly for England and let myself and my team down. I just needed a little time to ease my niggles. I then put in a good performance for Bath in front of a watching Clive, which seemed to do the trick. I'm just happy to have the shirt back. It's a huge relief because whenever you lose your place for any reason you always wonder whether your window has just been closed for good.'

On the bench, the major development was the promotion of twenty-one-year-old Leicester centre Ollie Smith, who, if the game was going well against Italy, would almost certainly make his debut at some point. Smith had been a Tigers fan since the age of seven, and had spent much of his childhood watching the likes of Johnson and Back. His response to being selected for the international team they had graced for so long was an understandable 'I'm pretty shocked.'

The squad was a ringing endorsement of the raised standards evident in the Zurich Premiership. Eleven of the twelve clubs were represented, with Bristol being the odd ones out, but only because Phil Christophers had returned to A-team duties. Two of the reinstated forwards underlined the exceptional competition for places these days within English rugby that has helped to catapult England to the top of the world rankings. Danny Grewcock understood the score. Although no player is indispensable, captain Johnson was virtually impossible to remove. 'The reason why I'm playing is because Johnno is injured,' admitted Grewcock. 'I very much appreciate that, but my priority still has to be to go out and play as well as I possibly can. We have to be on our mettle every time we play. Clive picks the team on form and it's the same for every player, but Johnno is a great player because he never has bad games. There is probably not a player who can match his achievements.'

Joe Worsley was in the side because both Neil Back and Lewis Moody were injured, but the Wasps flanker rightly saw this as his chance. 'I'd never consider I'm keeping the place warm for someone else,' he said. 'Otherwise I'd give it up and do something else. You have to believe you deserve to be there. The minute you don't you would be out of the window. There are six or seven back-row forwards who all believe they can do it. Clive came home from our tour to Argentina last year in the knowledge that he had a squad of thirty players, all of whom could play. Any change wouldn't weaken the side. We could almost have fifteen injuries and have an entirely different team out and we would still have a really good side.'

That was a fact not lost on Italy's coach, John Kirwan. Still, he was hoping that the doom-mongers predicting an avalanche of English points would be proved wrong. Two years earlier, Italy had been hit for eighty points at Twickenham. This time, on the basis of a win over Wales and a spirited display against Ireland, the former New Zealand back was expecting a better scoreline. 'We now have staff working overtime,' he explained the day before the game. 'I had no doubts about taking over the Italian job. I live there, I am part of it and I know how they approach life. The players are fantastic with things that happen to them that you would not normally see in other parts of the rugby world.'

His lock, Marco Bortolami, certainly seemed to believe that Kirwan was just the job. 'John's done wonders for us,' he said. 'Since he came, the feeling in the Italian camp has completely changed. He is instilling a sense of belief in us. We go into the game with the belief and courage to express ourselves.'

As the game would be staged on Sunday, both England and Italy had the luxury of watching Ireland scrape home against France at Lansdowne Road, and Scotland beat Wales at Murrayfield. The Irish win meant that they, too, were homing in on a possible Grand Slam. To achieve this, however, they would need to beat England on the last day of the tournament, something not lost on Clive Woodward. 'I do hope we get another crack at the Grand Slam against Ireland,' he said.' We have two games to go before then,

however. There's no point in looking back. What's done is done. As a group of players and coaches you just hope the experiences, good and bad, put you in a better state so that one day we actually win this thing.'

He and his England team would take one more vital step towards fulfilling their dream twenty-four hours later, but it was far from the stroll that most had predicted, in spite of an avalanche of early English scoring. Perhaps the team lost concentration. After all, to be 33–0 up after twenty-two minutes left a great deal of the game to be played in the knowledge that it was already won. The team's organisation was also disrupted by a series of substitutions – seven in all – and injuries to new captain Wilkinson and his replacement Hodgson. The non-essential substitutions could be justified in that they gave everyone a run-out in this crucial World Cup year, but the fact remained that England were forced to defend for three-quarters of the match against an unbowed Italy. At the final reckoning, although the overall

BELOW Jonny kicks from the halfway line.

scoreline suggested a home romp, anyone who had been at Twickenham knew different, and perhaps a more accurate picture of the match is revealed by the score for the last hour, which England shaded, 7–5.

On the plus side, and there *were* many pluses, was the performance of Josh Lewsey, who, finally given his chance to play for England at Twickenham, seized it with both hands. Of the five early first-half tries, Lewsey scored two (the first and the fourth) and laid on two more for James Simpson-Daniel (the third) and Mike Tindall (the fifth). If Lewsey's first, after just three minutes, was a relatively simple finish on the wing after a flowing backs' move, his second was as good an individual try as you could wish to see. Seeing the narrowest of holes in the Italian defence Lewsey cut through two opponents, looked up, and saw a sixty-five-metre run to the Italian line. In front of him, too, stood Mirco Bergamasco. No matter, Lewsey bamboozled Italy's last line of defence with a corkscrew run at pace that turned the full-back inside out before touching down close enough to the posts to make Wilkinson's job easy with the conversion. It was a try that, barring injury, probably nailed down his place in the England World Cup squad to be named in the autumn. He had proved to every other player seeming-

ABOVE AND RIGHT James Simpson-Daniel en route to scoring a try versus Italy.

ABOVE Steve Thompson scores
his first international try.

RIGHT Simpson-Daniel held up
by determined Italian defence.

ABOVE Lewsey completes a wonderful solo try.

LEFT Josh Lewsey enjoys a sensational Twickenham debut.

ly on the periphery of the squad that advances can be made if chances are taken.

'From a personal point of view the game couldn't have gone any better for me,' Lewsey said. 'When you have the likes of Wilkinson, Greenwood and Tindall playing, no wonder the England back three can look good. The first try was pretty simple by the time the ball got to me. Simpson-Daniel's pass was a little high, but any player worth his salt would expect to catch and score from there. It was my first touch of the ball, however, and it not only gave me a lot of confidence but meant that I could enjoy the rest of the game. I felt as if the pressure was off.

'For the second try, I filled in at ten in place of Jonny and noticed that our other backs were drawing so much attention that the Italian defence was flat with a gap in front of me. Once I'd burst through, my first reaction was to look

for support, but because we were flat too there was no one near me. Their full-back invited me to run at him, so I did. Afterwards Clive Woodward told me: "If you're going to score a try like that, then you are entitled to celebrate more," but that's not really my style. Some of that try came from my sevens experience and, in fact, Joe Lydon, the sevens manager, telephoned me straight after the game to tell me he'd seen me score an identical try playing for his England sevens team. Shaun Edwards at Wasps always goes on about making sure we ground the ball properly, which is why I gave it such a big hug like a teddy bear.'

The second try of the day was scored by the ever-impressive Steve Thompson, who ploughed through three Italian shirts from five yards out after Matt Dawson's initial surge. James Simpson-Daniel was the grateful recipient of another free-flowing exchange of passes along the backs line to score England's third. The points were coming so thick and fast for England at this stage that the confused Twickenham scoreboard momentarily flashed up Daniel Simpson as the scorer. Tindall finished off a well-worked blindside move

for his try, England's fifth. 'Those first twenty minutes were how you envisage rugby should be played,' Tindall said. 'I'd take a try any day playing for England, no matter who against or in what situation. The way we were playing, we deserved to be putting points on the board but, for me, after being dropped, it felt like my first try for England in my first game.'

At this stage, England had scored a point every thirty-nine seconds. Italy were staring at a hiding that would have done the Six Nations no favours at all, as well as ruining the recent advances they had made. In their defence, they had not played badly. They had merely been unfortunate enough to be on the receiving end of a twenty-minute onslaught of some of the finest rugby ever witnessed at headquarters. 'I was very aware that there was every chance of a downturn in the game from our point of view,' said Wilkinson. 'Having raced away to such an impressive lead, I knew it would be tough to maintain it, and it was also not a fair reflection on Italy. They are a better side than the first twenty minutes suggested.'

Lesser teams may have given up the ghost by then. Indeed, Italy themselves two years before had let their heads drop and allowed England free passage. This time, however, and to their enormous credit, they dug in their heels. And as they began to hit back with a series of attacks and long periods of possession, so England's performance, hitherto scintillating, became ragged. The post-match statistics revealed that England had been forced to make 171 tackles to Italy's 109, had conceded 15 penalties to Italy's 9, and had faced 140 carries from the Azzurri while launching only 109 themselves.

It was an astonishing transformation in all respects save for the crucial one: points. Despite all of Italy's territorial and possession advantage, they could manage only one try, scored by Mirco Bergamasco in the 58th minute after a polished set of passes sent the full-back clear in the corner.

By then Wilkinson had left the fray. 'I had a big reaction in my right shoulder after a tackle,' he said. 'I was very upset to leave the field for three reasons: I hate leaving the field in any circumstances; this was worse because I was captain; and I wanted to stay to help improve the situation.'

LEFT Mike Tindall touches down on his return to the England fold.

RIGHT Dan Luger makes the most of re-selection to the England starting fifteen.

His replacement Hodgson's injury, to his left knee, seemed even more serious. For the Sale Shark, sidelined only six minutes after replacing Wilkinson, a visit to a specialist the following day would follow amid concerns that he had severe ligament damage. 'I suffered the injury after just two minutes,' Hodgson explained. 'I had the ball in my hands and stepped up on my left leg. I felt it go immediately and thought it was serious. But because I wasn't in absolute agony I felt I might be able to run it off. With Jonny off the field already it was important I remained in the game, but it soon became obvious I couldn't carry on.'

As a result of all this injury mayhem, England, now under the leadership of Dallaglio, would finish the game with Will Greenwood standing in at fly-half, debutant Ollie Smith at outside centre, reserve scrum-half Kyran Bracken on the left wing and Simpson-Daniel at full-back after man-of-the-match Lewsey had been withdrawn ten minutes before time. Moments after Lewsey's departure England scored their sixth try of the afternoon with just about their only attack of the second half. Smith, revealing

all the hallmarks of a future regular in the England set-up, burst through the Italian defence before releasing Dan Luger with a perfectly weighted pass to score in the corner. Luger, normally so ebullient when he scores, did not even bother with his customary salute to the crowd. 'To be honest, I didn't really enjoy the game,' he explained. 'We'd won it after twenty-odd minutes and I was still under a lot of personal pressure coming to terms with Nick Duncombe's death. I was also coming back from injury and didn't feel I'd had a particularly good game.'

Afterwards there was a good deal of head-scratching. 'Obviously, the remainder of the game didn't go as well as the first twenty,' conceded England Head Coach Woodward. 'You have to take your hat off to the Italian team. The way they came back and dominated the rest of the game was pretty impressive. They could have folded but did the complete opposite and I went into their dressing-room to say well done. They played some great stuff but we were never going to lose after that start. Unfortunately, the rest of the match overshadowed the first twenty minutes.'

ABOVE Glad I'm not in there: Jonny surveys the forwards at work.

The forwards' coach Andy Robinson concurred. 'They tired us out a bit because of the amount of defensive work we had to do,' he admitted. 'We're disappointed by the number of knock-ons, dropped passes and loss of line-out ball. The biggest problem was that our line-out didn't function as well as we would have liked.'

Lawrence Dallaglio said: 'I thought there was a tendency at 33–0 to do things we weren't doing in the first twenty minutes. But there are an enormous number of players playing well and it's difficult to know who your best team is now.'

Will Greenwood was not unduly concerned. 'If it had been a boxing match it would have been over after two rounds,' he said. 'Italy did very well in the second half but you've got to turn up at the start. It's no good playing good rugby after forty minutes when you're 33–0 down.'

The Italians took great heart from their comeback, but also rued their early form. 'I knew we were better than the way we started,' said coach John Kirwan. 'I sent messages out not to kick the ball away. We can't wait for twenty minutes until we start playing. We must go on the field as equals. We had a goal of coming off the field with heads held high and, for achieving that, I'm proud of them.' His captain, Alessandro Troncon, added: 'The emotion and the atmosphere were too much for us at the beginning, but we matured as the game went on.'

Nevertheless, in spite of the fight of the Italians and England's lacklustre second-half display, it was the latter who were now only 160 minutes away from the Grand

LEFT Charlie Hodgson, on the pitch for only six minutes, gets to grips with Aaron Persico.

BELOW Ollie Smith makes his mark on his debut.

Slam. 'That's three wins out of three,' Wilkinson reminded everyone. 'For me, it has been a fantastic day, a privilege and an honour. I'm disappointed that we fell some way short of our high standards in the second half of the game, but I will still look back on this day with enormous happiness and great memories.'

There was also much relief that Wilkinson's injury did not seem to be too serious, and he expected to be fit to face Scotland in the Calcutta Cup at Twickenham. Stage four of the Grand Slam attempt was a fortnight away – plenty of time for injuries to heal, and lessons to be learned from the last hour of the match against Italy. England had been far from satisfied in each of their three wins to date. It was time to perform at their best.

ENGLAND 40
SCOTLAND 9

Saturday, 22 March 2003 at Twickenham

ENGLAND

Lewsey, Robinson, Greenwood, Tindall (Luger, 56), Cohen, Wilkinson (Grayson, 66), Dawson, Rowntree (Woodman, 66), Thompson, Leonard, Johnson, Kay (Grewcock, 62), Hill, Back, Dallaglio (J. Worsley, 74). SUBS (not used): Regan, Gomarsall

Tries

Robinson 2, Lewsey, Cohen

Conversions

Wilkinson 3, Grayson

Penalties

Wilkinson 4

SCOTLAND

Metcalfe, Paterson, McLaren (Utterson, 56), Craig, Logan, Townsend, Redpath, Smith, Bulloch, Douglas (Kerr, 72), Murray (Grimes, 51), Hines, White, Mower (Beattie, 67), Taylor SUBS (not used): Russell, Blair, Ross

Penalties

Paterson 3

Referee

Alan Lewis (Ireland)

Attendance

75,000

'…it's always exciting knowing that you're about to face the Scots'

Clive Woodward's worst fears concerning Charlie Hodgson were confirmed two days after the Italy game. An MRI scan revealed that the Sale Shark had indeed ruptured the cruciate ligament in his left knee. This meant that he was out of the forthcoming Calcutta Cup match, the rest of the Six Nations tournament, England's two-test June tour in New Zealand and Australia, and quite possibly the World Cup, too. 'Charlie is a huge, huge loss to us,' a disappointed Woodward reported. 'Potentially I was going to start Charlie for the Scotland game and give Jonny Wilkinson a weekend off. I hope he makes a speedy and full recovery. His injury overshadowed the whole day for me.'

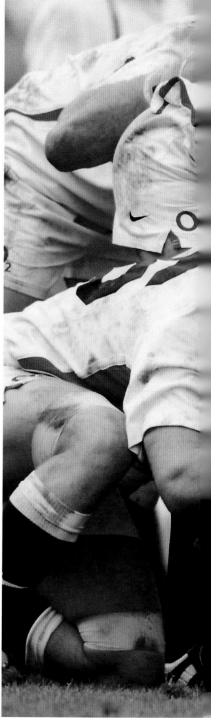

ABOVE England's backs
practise their kicks.

RIGHT Jason Leonard, Steve
Thompson, Graham Rowntree:
a formidable England front row.

Hodgson had prepared himself for the worst. 'In the back of my mind I was hoping it was not that serious because other people with the injury I sustained screamed in pain at the time while I did not. But missing the autumn internationals when I'd injured the other leg seemed to keep me philosophical about it all. When I heard I'd completely torn my ligaments I took the news much better than I would have expected.'

The other major talking point in the aftermath of the Italian win was what Woodward would do with Josh Lewsey. After the full-back's two-try Six Nations debut, the Head Coach was left with the kind of selection dilemma every coach desires. Should he drop Lewsey to the bench to accommodate Jason Robinson, who would be available for selection after recovering from injury. Would he play both Robinson and Lewsey? If so, who would play at full-back, and who would start out on the wing? Could he perhaps play one or the other in the centre? Or would he decide on the previously unthinkable and decide that Lewsey's Italian display should force

Robinson to the bench? The fact that Woodward made a point of singling out Mike Tindall, as well as prop Graham Rowntree, for praise after the win over Italy suggested that he would not be considering either Robinson or Lewsey at outside centre. But there were still all of the other permutations.

'Josh made a powerful case for himself,' argued his Wasps teammate, Lawrence Dallaglio. 'He has given the management a real selection headache,' added James Simpson-Daniel. 'Josh made a big difference when he hit the line,' chipped in Matt Dawson. 'He really put authority on the game,' explained Jonny Wilkinson.

A happy Clive Woodward accepted his dilemma. 'It's a good debate and a healthy debate,' he said. 'From my point of view, I'm just glad he's in the team. I'm relaxed about wherever he plays. He is a fantastic player, whether at full-back, wing or centre.'

A week later the England Head Coach came up with an answer as he announced a heavyweight team that contained the usual surprises. Lewsey, who would probably have been out in the Gulf with his army colleagues in the Desert Rats but for his decision to give full-time rugby a go, retained his number-fifteen shirt. In the process, arguably England's most potent attacking force, Jason

Robinson, having played at full-back for the past fifteen months, would switch to his original right wing. Although it had been some time since he had last appeared there, the impact he made as a British and Irish Lion back in 2001, let alone the 171 tries and 15 trophies he won in the position during his nine years playing rugby league, left no cause for concern.

There had been concern over the former Wigan star's fitness, however, but this had vanished after a first-class display for Sale against Leeds. 'I watched Jason's performance on television and he was absolutely awesome,' Lewsey stated. 'If he had a point to prove, he certainly proved it. He

was quite amazing and I couldn't afford to build myself up and count any chickens in case of disappointment.'

As a result, Woodward's choice was not, as had been expected, between Robinson and Lewsey, but between Robinson and Dan Luger. 'I've always said that as long as we have a full-back of real quality I am very happy to play Jason on the wing,' the England Head Coach confirmed. 'I don't care where Jason Robinson plays as long as he is out there. We'll give him a free role.' Technically, Robinson would replace Simpson-Daniel on the right, with Ben Cohen, now also fully fit, taking Luger's place on the left. The Harlequins wing would revert to the bench.

As for Lewsey, Woodward threw down the gauntlet for his latest star. 'This is the first time that Josh has pushed a big name on to the replacement bench,' he said. 'It will be a big test for him. He has the shirt and he is in the position, but there will be a lot more pressure on him against Scotland.'

LEFT Will Greenwood
in full flow.

dredth cap against France, found himself straight back in the starting line-up, albeit in the less familiar role of tight-head prop. He had not played a minute of competitive rugby since the injury five weeks previously, but would nevertheless begin an unprecedented fourteenth Calcutta Cup. This was some achievement, especially as the medical prognosis for his muscle tear was ten weeks out of the game.

ABOVE Not much gets
past Martin Johnson.

In the forwards there were wholesale changes due to the return of three heavyweight hitters. Martin Johnson, as expected, reclaimed his captaincy from Wilkinson, along with his place in the second row from Danny Grewcock. Neil Back's recovery from a troublesome calf injury meant a revival of the familiar back-row threesome of Back, Dallaglio and Hill, and a return to the bench for Joe Worsley. And Jason Leonard, having just about recovered from his hamstring tear sustained while winning his hun-

England had been resigned to seeing out the Six Nations without the services of their evergreen prop, but Leonard, typically, defied expert opinion by recovering in half the predicted time. 'I trust all these players implicitly, none more so than Leonard,' Woodward explained. 'He says he's fit so I had no hesitation in picking him. He's done brilliantly to recover so quickly. How he's done it is something you'd better ask his mates at The Sun in Richmond.'

This affectionate dig at the prop's previous penchant for a pint or two was quickly refuted by the man beginning his second ton of caps. 'I've stayed out of the pubs and I've been whiter than white,' he insisted. 'I don't think I've ever worked so hard in all my life as I have in the past few weeks. I've trained exceptionally hard in the past four weeks and exceeded all my expectations. Originally I thought I might

get back for the last match against Ireland and only then with a bit of luck. The physios with Harlequins and England have been absolutely killing me these last ten days. They've done everything to make sure my hamstring is one hundred per cent. I don't know what more they could have done short of chopping the bloody thing off. I'm happy to say I've come through every test.'

His switch to tighthead guaranteed him a testing return against Tom Smith, the Scottish loosehead who had ousted him from the test team on the last two Lions tours. 'Tom's one of the best props in the world and I know him better than most,' Leonard revealed. 'Take it from me, I won't be holding back.'

The removal of Hodgson from the cause meant that, even though Woodward had been considering keeping Wilkinson in reserve, the prospect was now out of the

question. By the Tuesday before the Calcutta Cup, the England Head Coach had decided that 'The Six Nations Championship is no time for experiment. Jonny's fit and fine. Not to pick him would send out the wrong message to the rest of the team, to the championship and to Scotland. This is arguably the strongest side I've put out in the championship.'

With Hodgson out of the reckoning, Woodward made one of his more interesting call-ups to the bench. Paul Grayson, the Northampton stand-off, thought his international days were long gone, having last appeared in an England shirt during the 1999 World Cup quarter-final defeat at the hands of South Africa. Most felt that, at thirty-one, he was leaning more towards coaching, but the arrival of former All Blacks coach Wayne Smith at Franklins Gardens had revitalised Grayson's career to the extent that Woodward had no qualms about recalling him to the English fold. 'I can't speak highly enough of Paul Grayson,' the England Head Coach stated. 'He's there on merit and was in line behind Jonny and Charlie.'

A day later Josh Lewsey, whose rise to eminence had been staggering, revealed his particular source of motivation for the 120th Calcutta Cup. 'Getting four letters from guys out in the Gulf yesterday wishing me luck means an incredible amount to me, particularly at this time,' Lewsey said. 'When you have got guys you have been through good and bad times with taking time out to do that, it is very humbling. It also brings home the reality of what's going on and how close it is. I have sent letters back but I don't know whether they will get them before or after the conflict begins, so I intend for my performance to let them know what their support means to me.

'This is a very big game for me, but the conflict puts everything into perspective. They are doing something over there that is really serious. I feel almost a part of that because many of them are very good friends of mine and my thoughts, certainly in the next couple of days, will be with them. Whenever I feel slightly tired, I think: Hang on a second, remember what you're doing here, who you're representing. We are representing all those guys out

BELOW Lewsey scores for the second successive Six Nations international.

there. They have got a job to do over there in the same way that we have got a job to do over here. That is one of the things that pushes me as a professional. You are representing a lot of people in a lot of jobs, not just in the war environment. When you pull on that shirt it means a lot to a lot of people.'

Scotland, meanwhile, decided their only chance might be to test out an English pack that was considerably older than their own eight men. There may have been over 400

ABOVE Mike Tindall cements his place in the England centres.

ABOVE RIGHT Tindall brought down close to the Scottish line.

caps between the English forwards, but the average age of the pack, now not including the relatively young Phil Vickery and Lewis Moody, was thirty, some four years older than the Scots. 'Six of their pack are over thirty,' argued Jim Telfer, Scotland's director of rugby. 'Having younger forwards can work to our advantage.' With this in mind, they promoted the abrasive, Australian-born lock Nathan Hines to their ranks.

This view, of course, served only to fire up the English

Then there was the prospect of a Grand Slam show-down against Ireland, just eighty minutes away, assuming England could see off the Scots and Ireland could win in Cardiff. Past defeats, however, had hardened the English to their more immediate cause. 'The environment is such that, if I don't play well as an individual, or if any of the guys don't play well, then we won't be picked against Ireland,' Lawrence Dallaglio reasoned. 'That's your best way of not thinking about Ireland. In time terms, that

pack. 'The forwards have taken those words on board,' said Woodward. 'They are looking forward to seeing the old legs running around as usual.'

Possibly a bigger threat to England came from Scotland's backs, who had not yet fired on all cylinders but boasted a number of game-breakers. The half-back pairing of Bryan Redpath and Gregor Townsend was a potential threat to any side in the world, while Chris Paterson and Glenn Metcalfe posed danger out on the wing and from full-back.

game is not long away. But in rugby terms, it's a long, long way away.'

Matt Dawson knows a thing or two about losing to the Scots after captaining England to defeat in the Murrayfield sleet in 2000. He was in an understandably cautious mood on the eve of the game: 'I don't know of any side in world rugby who raise their game against England as much as the Scots. No matter what sort of form they are showing, they rarely fail to put in a big dis-

play against us. The old rivalry is very special and there is usually a real edge to games between the two sides, so we need to hit the ground running.'

There had been something of an extra spring in England captain Martin Johnson's step all week. This, so his team-mates believed, was down to the fact that on the night that England had beaten Italy a fortnight before he had become a father for the first time, after his wife, Kay, had given birth to daughter Molly. 'It was a wonderful thing to happen, of course, but the main reason why I've been energetic in training is because the break from rugby for a week did me a lot of good,' asid Johnson. 'My niggles have cleared up and I missed playing for England. It's been good to be back, and it's always exciting knowing that you're about to face the Scots.'

Twenty-four hours later England had taken their fourth step towards the Grand Slam by dismissing a redoubtable Scotland to claim the Calcutta Cup and record an incredible twenty-first straight win at Twickenham. In doing so they produced their best display of the Six Nations tournament to date. Much of it, again, was down to Josh Lewsey, as well as the man he replaced at full-back, Jason Robinson.

ABOVE Ben Cohen seizes on Bryan Redpath's error to score the easiest try of his test career.

The latter, starting on the right wing before shifting to outside centre after an injury reshuffle in the second half, was especially devastating. Three tries from this pairing, plus the usual impeccable kicking display from Jonny Wilkinson, who landed seven out of seven, destroyed Scotland.

Two Wilkinson penalties inside the first eleven minutes provided a six-point cushion in this 120th edition of the oldest international in rugby, but Scotland, encouraged by their win over Wales the fortnight before and fielding a tough, uncompromising line-up, refused to lie down and accept what most of the 75,000 crowd saw as inevitable. Their mini-revival followed a bizarre series of yellow cards that saw Scotland reduced to thirteen men, and then England losing the services of Robinson for ten minutes.

First to leave the field was Scotland's Australian-born flanker, Andrew Mower, dismissed for taking out Mike Tindall while the Bath centre was in mid-air catching the

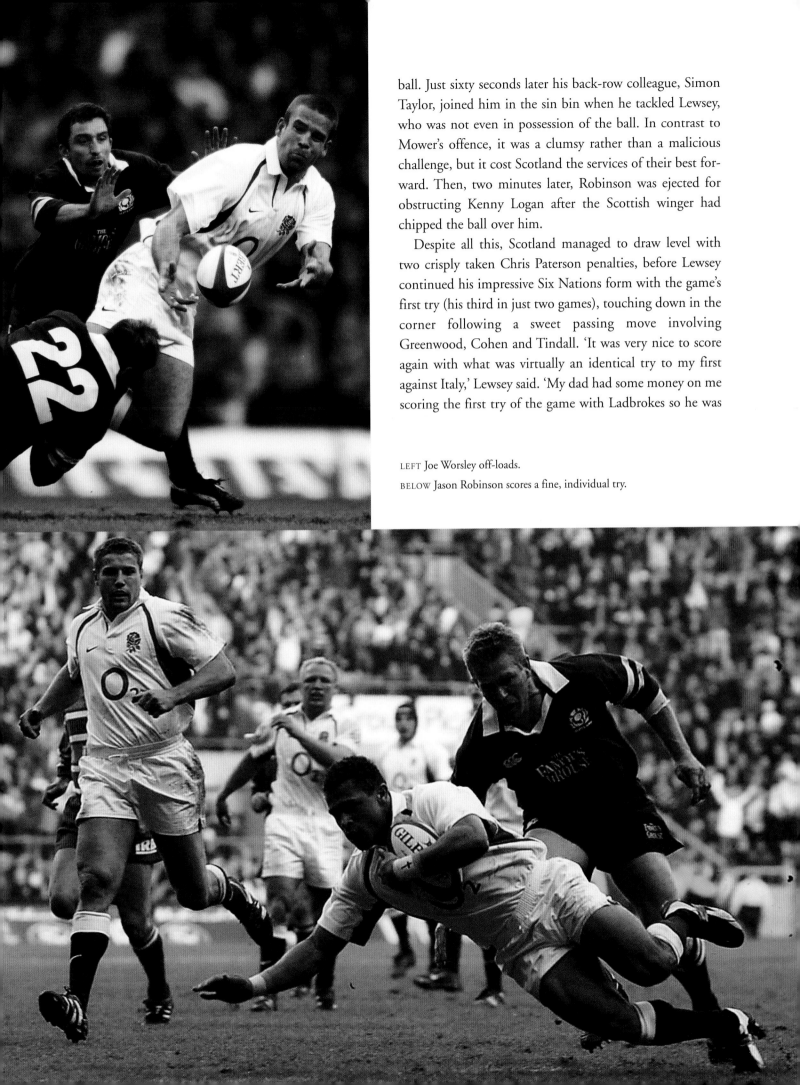

ball. Just sixty seconds later his back-row colleague, Simon Taylor, joined him in the sin bin when he tackled Lewsey, who was not even in possession of the ball. In contrast to Mower's offence, it was a clumsy rather than a malicious challenge, but it cost Scotland the services of their best forward. Then, two minutes later, Robinson was ejected for obstructing Kenny Logan after the Scottish winger had chipped the ball over him.

Despite all this, Scotland managed to draw level with two crisply taken Chris Paterson penalties, before Lewsey continued his impressive Six Nations form with the game's first try (his third in just two games), touching down in the corner following a sweet passing move involving Greenwood, Cohen and Tindall. 'It was very nice to score again with what was virtually an identical try to my first against Italy,' Lewsey said. 'My dad had some money on me scoring the first try of the game with Ladbrokes so he was

LEFT Joe Worsley off-loads.

BELOW Jason Robinson scores a fine, individual try.

ABOVE Robinson again, in an identikit try to that scored against France.

very happy on two counts. Like against Italy, all I had to do was flop over the line. The try was created by great hands from Will Greenwood and Ben Cohen. As my brother kindly told me later, my dad could have finished off the move, let alone me.'

Back came Scotland, enjoying more of the first-half possession and territory, with Paterson striking a third successful penalty, before Wilkinson restored England's advantage with his third penalty of the afternoon just before half-time. The 16–9 lead was a useful foundation, but it had not been the performance England had planned. In the second half, however, they immediately upped the ante when a period of sustained pressure saw them laying siege to the Scottish line.

Ben Cohen had a try ruled out following a cross-field punt from Wilkinson. The referee, Alan Lewis, judged that Cohen had knocked the ball forward when television replays showed clearly that the ball had fallen behind the wing. 'I was really annoyed about that decision, partly because it was my first game back from injury having missed the Italy game, and also because I made a big effort to make sure that if I dropped the ball, it would fall behind me,' explained Cohen. 'I couldn't believe it when the try wasn't given. I couldn't understand why the try could not have been referred to the video referee.'

It made little difference. From the ensuing scrum

Scotland captain Bryan Redpath was tackled by Matt Dawson just as he was attempting to clear. The ball squirmed out and straight to a grateful Cohen, who scooped it up and touched down over the line two metres ahead for his twentieth international try. 'Matt has to take all the credit for the try,' Cohen insisted. 'He put enormous pressure on Redpath to make the error, and all I had to do was pick up the ball and fall over the line. I'm happy to do that all day.'

Once Wilkinson had converted and then added a further penalty four minutes later, England had stretched the lead to 26–9 and there was no way back for the Scots. With an injured Tindall replaced by Dan Luger, Robinson moved into the centre with immediate effect. His speed off the mark would wreak havoc in the tiring Scottish defence. A quick tap penalty from Matt Dawson in the 64th minute, a pass that looked suspiciously as if it were meant for Neil Back, and Robinson, having plucked the ball out of the sky, was off through a tiny gap. Away he sped: a jink left Gordon Bulloch stranded and then Glenn Metcalfe, no slouch himself, fell by the wayside as Robinson roared over to score.

There was still time, three minutes before the end, for

Robinson to score a second under the posts, collecting from just a few yards out after a typical sniping break from Dawson and a trademark one-handed pass towards the full-back, turned winger, turned centre.

If the first half had been a little patchy by England's high standards, the second had been much more effective, with twenty-four unanswered points and three gloriously worked tries. Once again it had been the opening fifteen minutes of the second half, a period of English dominance in all their 2002/3 games save for Italy, that knocked the stuffing out of Scotland. Lewsey was playing as if he had always worn the number-fifteen shirt. Robinson proved that he is a danger wherever he plays. Tindall, responding in the best way to recent criticism, knocked huge dents into the Scottish defence and provided space for others to exploit., Dawson was the supplier for both of Robinson's tries, and his tackle on Redpath set up Cohen for his score. Wilkinson helped himself to eighteen points. In other words, the backs were outstanding.

Dawson's day ended painfully, though, when a stray boot from teammate Richard Hill caught the bridge of his nose in a freak accident. Blood immediately began to pump from the scrum-half's wound. 'I can't deny it hurt a little, but the doc did a brilliant job patching me up with thirteen stitches afterwards,' Dawson revealed. 'Any chance of breaking into the modelling world has probably gone for ever, but at least I am one hundred per cent fit to play whatever role is required of me.'

The consensus of opinion was that a hard day's work had been carried out well. Clive Woodward was especially delighted by how well Robinson had returned to the set-up. 'It makes no difference where Jason Robinson plays because he can score from anywhere,' the Head Coach said. 'I'm only glad he plays in a white jersey.' Robinson, with four tries now to his name in just three Calcutta Cup games, said, 'I always enjoy playing against the Scots. Being sent to the sin bin did motivate me and I was determined to make up for it.'

Others had their say, too. 'We were a little frustrated but still had a good victory,' opined Lewsey. 'A lot of credit has to go to Scotland. They came out and played some good rugby. We made some unforced errors and it means we have still got some work to do.' Mike Tindall's view was similar: 'It was a frustrating game because the Scots spoiled really well. They came up very fast and put pressure on our first two receivers. We had to generate fast ball to keep the Scots from getting in

our faces.' Steve Thompson added: 'Scotland are a very physical team. We kept running at them and wore them down in the end.' His Northampton colleague Dawson was rightly happy with the day's work. 'A very satisfying win and probably our most complete performance of the championship so far,' he said. 'It was a very content England changing-room afterwards.' And Neil Back was equally pleased: 'Everyone else was looking ahead to Ireland and saw this game as nothing more than a stepping stone which we'd easily walk over. That made it potentially difficult for us. I thought our attitude was excellent. We remained completely focused on this game and nothing else.'

The time to enjoy another Calcutta Cup victory would be short-lived. Over in Cardiff earlier that same afternoon an injury-time drop goal from Ronan O'Gara had snatched a narrow victory over Wales to set everything up for a winner-takes-all Grand Slam decider in Dublin in eight days' time. Everything – the Slam, the Six Nations title, the Triple Crown and the chance for England to avenge the defeat in Dublin in 2001 – would be up for grabs. Eight long and frustrating years waiting for the Slam could finally be over.

For Ireland, perhaps the stakes were even higher. They looked more than ready to take on the English, and to win their first Grand Slam for fifty-five years.

For now, the World Cup could wait.

ABOVE With four tries in just three
Calcutta Cup games, Jason Robinson
is again Man of the Match.

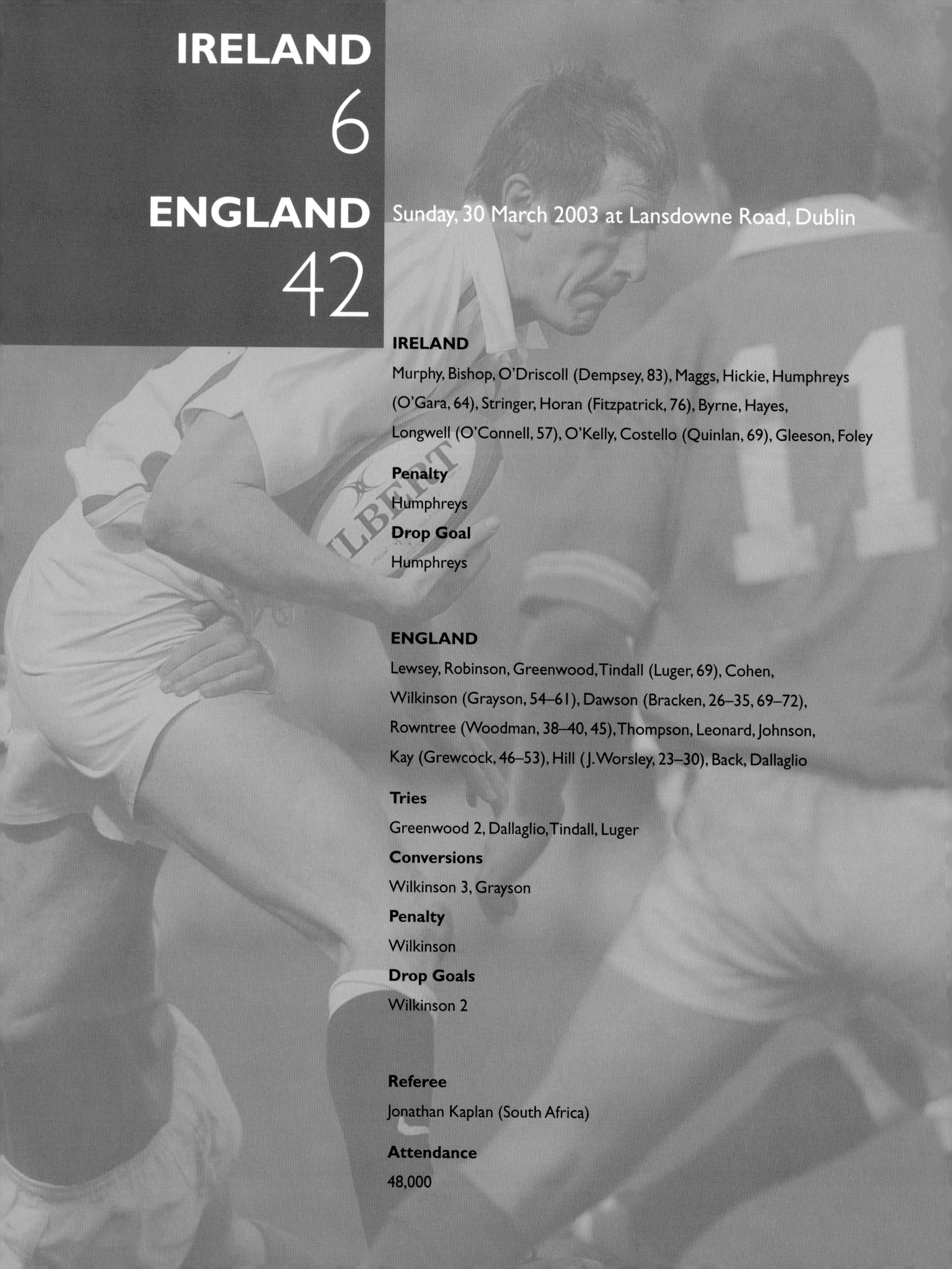

IRELAND 6
ENGLAND 42

Sunday, 30 March 2003 at Lansdowne Road, Dublin

IRELAND

Murphy, Bishop, O'Driscoll (Dempsey, 83), Maggs, Hickie, Humphreys (O'Gara, 64), Stringer, Horan (Fitzpatrick, 76), Byrne, Hayes, Longwell (O'Connell, 57), O'Kelly, Costello (Quinlan, 69), Gleeson, Foley

Penalty

Humphreys

Drop Goal

Humphreys

ENGLAND

Lewsey, Robinson, Greenwood, Tindall (Luger, 69), Cohen, Wilkinson (Grayson, 54–61), Dawson (Bracken, 26–35, 69–72), Rowntree (Woodman, 38–40, 45), Thompson, Leonard, Johnson, Kay (Grewcock, 46–53), Hill (J. Worsley, 23–30), Back, Dallaglio

Tries

Greenwood 2, Dallaglio, Tindall, Luger

Conversions

Wilkinson 3, Grayson

Penalty

Wilkinson

Drop Goals

Wilkinson 2

Referee

Jonathan Kaplan (South Africa)

Attendance

48,000

CHAPTER EIGHT

'The number-one team in the world showed us why they are that today'

For Martin Johnson, this was one of the most exciting times of his life. Just a fortnight earlier he had become a father, and now he was ready to lead England out in Dublin to face their destiny. Ask Johnson about his importance to the team and he dismisses the notion. Ask anyone else and they will argue that the man is vital. Was it really a coincidence that on the three previous attempts to win the Grand Slam on the final day of the Six Nations Johnson had been missing?

He had already experienced the joy of winning the Slam, back in 1995, when he was a young lock playing under the leadership of Will Carling. Eight long years had passed since then. The Leicester captain had subsequently led the British and Irish Lions to victory in South Africa in 1997 and to narrow defeat in Australia in 2001, as well as skippering

England to the 2001 Six Nations title (he was injured for the 2000 tournament), but the Slam under his captaincy had eluded him.

The birth of Molly Johnson had brought some welcome perspective into his life at just the right time. 'She has made me realise that things aren't here for ever and that I should enjoy the moment while I can,' the thirty-three-year-old revealed on the Monday after the Calcutta Cup, his one day

off to recuperate before rejoining the England squad for the Irish showdown six days later. 'Suddenly, my priorities and responsibilities have changed. She's my number-one concern, now.' She had already witnessed her father in action as she had joined her mother to watch England beat the Scots at Twickenham. 'Molly slept for much of the game and apparently cried during "Flower of Scotland",' he reported.

Johnson was under no illusions regarding the importance of the forthcoming match, nor of each team's aspirations. 'Either side would take a 3–0 win right now, I can promise you,' he insisted. 'In fact, I'd grab a one-point victory any day. Whatever it takes, penalties, drop-goals, anything. All we have to do is win, nothing more, nothing less. I don't care how we achieve it. I don't care how badly we play, just as long as we emerge the winners. People use the phrase "must-win games" all the time, but this is just about as "must-win" as you can get.

'It would be a massive relief to win and a huge weight off our shoulders. No matter what this side have achieved over the years, we've never won the Grand Slam. That's a huge failing to our name. We're absolutely desperate to win it this time. Above all else, we want to win it for ourselves.'

The memory of defeat eighteen months before at Lansdowne Road also stuck in the craw. Johnson missed the game with a broken hand but joined his defeated teammates on the pitch to collect the Six Nations trophy as the Irish players danced and jigged their way around the ground on a lap of honour. 'It was truly bizarre standing there on the podium with the trophy and feeling so wretched,' Johnson recalled. 'We lost the game, no excuses. I wasn't going to come down from the stand if we'd won, but I thought I'd show my support. Looking back now, it wasn't the best of experiences for me. I don't intend to go through it again.'

Johnson was convinced that Sunday's game was going to be as tough an examination of England's credentials as anything they had experienced during the Six Nations or even in the three autumn internationals against the Southern Hemisphere. 'I've been saying from day one, when everyone kept on insisting our game against France at the start of the tournament would decide the outcome, that this test in Dublin would be the biggest game of the Six Nations. I'd even go as far as to say there is now a big six, not five, in international rugby. Ireland have joined the party. People say they scraped home against Wales at the weekend, but that was a difficult game for the Irish. The fact that they came through without playing particularly well speaks volumes for them.

'This will be the best Irish side we've ever prepared to play against. In terms of their consistency and their ability to win games, they are in better shape than ever before. They've got the chance to do something that they've not done in a long, long time. That's the challenge and we accept it. I certainly don't expect them to freeze or let the occasion get to them.

thoughts are focused on Sunday. This match is the culmination of four years' work. That's what it's boiled down to. The pressure to win this match and this Grand Slam comes from within. There are no more learning curves. Winning against Ireland is all that matters. I've not even thought of the ramifications if it weren't to go our way.

If anything, it will be just the opposite. They will probably be at their most enthusiastic and energetic. Of course, there will be pressure on them. But I don't anticipate them playing with anything but the commitment and skill they have shown all through the championship.

'It's going to be tough, a real battle between two very sound defences. We'll have to play for the full eighty minutes and, unlike the other games, we'll have to play for long periods without the ball. It might boil down to who cracks first.'

As the week unfolded so England, normally keen to play things down, were happy to acknowledge the enormity of the occasion in Dublin, and the pressure resting on their shoulders. On the Monday night, after naming the same fifteen that had started against Scotland, Head Coach Clive Woodward was in combative mood. 'Defeat?' he asked. 'It's not even entered my mind. Next Monday doesn't exist as far as I'm concerned. The World Cup doesn't exist. All our

'This weekend will give us the chance to bury the myth that we can't win away from home. We've no fears about playing away. It's a total myth to say we can't perform away from home. One of the reasons people argue this is because we're so good at Twickenham.

'Ireland will have to play well to beat us, and they are more than capable of doing that on the day. However, this group of players deserves a Grand Slam. They've taken English rugby to a new level. I'm desperate for them to get the Slam. As we've found over the years, it won't come easily. And, with Ireland going for it too, this is the hardest of all those chances.'

Such determination was mirrored in the attitudes of his senior players. 'I've been saying all season that it's important for this England side to win something tangible and I'm not about to back down from that now,' said Lawrence Dallaglio. 'Ultimately you're judged on what you win. A player's career is all about striving to be the best so, yes, if I were to finish my career without a Slam then I would feel unfulfilled. It's great to have another opportunity to have a crack at a Grand Slam. It's not one I intend to waste. It's a chance, also, to right a few wrongs.'

Neil Back had had the misfortune of playing in all three previous Grand Slam slip-ups, against Wales in 1999 at Wembley, Scotland a year later at Murrayfield, and Ireland in 2001 at Lansdowne Road. 'Winning a Slam is a massive personal goal,' said the flanker. 'I've set out my stall this year to win one. But none of us is uptight about it. That's one thing we have learned.'

Matt Dawson made a point in an intense week not to relive the past horrors of lost Grand Slam opportunities. 'I didn't want to talk about the previous defeats, I didn't want to read about them, and I certainly didn't want to have to watch them again,' he said. 'We had a video session during the week to remind us of where we'd failed in the past, and how we had to win this time. I kept my head down because I didn't need nor want to be reminded of it. The good thing is that I've become totally focused on the game and on my job. There is no motivational force of revenge, just an intention to be as ruthless and professional as possible.'

Will Greenwood acknowledged that the forthcoming match's significance had been heightened still further by

BELOW Jason Robinson is caught for once.

ABOVE Jonny Wilkinson says hello to Justin Bishop with a trademark hit.

the form of the opposition. 'We were all absolutely delighted when Ronan O'Gara's last-minute drop goal went over against Wales,' he explained. 'It placed both teams in a winner-takes-all situation. There are a lot of thirty-year-olds in the England team and, with it being World Cup year as well, this is just about the last chance for most of them. I have to ask myself, too, how many more cracks am I going to have at a Grand Slam? So we're placing pressure on ourselves. It's just like the Eminem song. One opportunity, one shot, one moment.'

The England players also knew the score when it came to their opponents. The Leicester contingent – Johnson, Back, Kay – had first-hand knowledge of the kind of damage their club colleague Geordan Murphy could inflict given half a chance. Those England members of the 2001 Lions team were also well aware of the threat posed by the Irish captain,

Brian O'Driscoll. Yet some of the less celebrated Irish backs caught the attention of Paul Grayson, on the bench again to cover for Jonny Wilkinson, and Mike Tindall. David Humphreys, for example, who had kept O'Gara sitting on the bench for much of the Six Nations tournament, was singled out. 'His decision-making is good,' said Grayson. 'And their tactics have proved successful. I do not know of many teams who play in their own half and, in terms of pure execution, Ireland do it as well as anybody.' Tindall agreed: 'They play great territory rugby. Humphreys is good at finding space with his boot and letting their chasing line do the rest.'

Kevin Maggs, the bulldozing centre who proves such a formidable foil for his captain, was also lauded. 'He has been brilliant for Ireland,' said Grayson. 'He always makes yards and is a real handful for the inside defender.' Tindall knew him well as a Bath teammate. 'Maggsy is an extra back-row man. He makes the hits and he wins the ball. He is part of a defence that gets in your face and shuts you down. If they

ABOVE Lawrence Dallaglio scores the crucial first try at Lansdowne Road.

catch you behind the gain line and turn the ball over, they are world class.'

The day before the game, on the Saturday afternoon while France were smashing Wales in Paris and Scotland were beating a spirited Italy in Edinburgh, Clive Woodward and Ireland's head coach Eddie O'Sullivan gave their final views before last-minute preparations. For Woodward, the fact that Johnson would be out there at Lansdowne Road was absolutely critical. 'I wouldn't swap Martin Johnson for any player in the world either to play or lead the team in this crucial game,' he insisted. 'It's a huge bonus to have him fully fit. He's a great player, a great captain and he's very, very experienced on the big occasions. You can't get bigger than this one and we know how much he wants to win the Slam for both himself as the captain and for his team. For many of the players it's going to be their last shot at the Slam. There's going to be no place to hide. It's not about excitement, it's about winning, and, believe me, a one-point victory will do.'

His words were echoed by his Irish counterpart, and by Ireland's captain. 'The build-up is like nothing I've ever experienced,' said O'Driscoll. 'The goodwill of the Irish people has been unbelievable. We see this as a one-off against England and a chance to win the Slam. We're relish-ing it.' O'Sullivan dismissed suggestions that Ireland's form had gone off the boil with their last-gasp win in Cardiff the week before. 'That was like a cup semi-final and we were full of nerves,' he explained. 'But now we're in the final. The history of the occasion is inspiring us and, although I make England the favourites, it's fifteen men against fifteen. It's all to play for.'

Indeed it was. The atmosphere prior to the arrival on the pitch of the two teams was electric. The Irish squad had already been treated to a private midweek concert by Christy Moore, the legendary singer of rebel songs. At Lansdowne Road Mick Galwey was then wheeled out to address the crowd before they sang all the Irish anthems more heartily than perhaps had ever been witnessed before in Dublin. It was, to say the least, an intimidating atmosphere. But England, with Matt Dawson winning his fiftieth cap, were unfazed. So determined was Martin Johnson to stand his ground throughout the afternoon that the day's proceedings began with an air of controversy. Having been led out to the right-hand side of a red carpet facing the main stand in order to meet the various dignitaries, including Irish President

Mary McAleese, and undergo the pre-match formalities, when asked to move over to the left to accommodate Ireland's 'lucky end' Johnson twice flatly refused. It led to an embarrassing sequence with the Irish team refusing to stand on the left as well, opting to line up on the grass to the right of England. 'With due respect to the Irish President, people don't come here to watch the presentations, they come here to watch a game of rugby,' said Johnson later. He had previously, during the warm-up routine, knocked over his own fitness adviser, Dave Reddin, which told you all you needed to know of the England captain's state of mind.

Neil Back had stuck his oar in over the pre-match situation as well. 'I was saying, "Stand firm, stand firm," when we were being asked to move,' he said. 'If we'd moved we would have given Ireland an immediate psychological edge. In the frame of mind that we were in, we weren't prepared to give them anything, not during the game, and not before either.'

It was a sign of things to come from the whole England team, although, early on, Ireland pressed hard. David Humphreys had already missed a long-range penalty attempt by a matter of inches when he landed a 4th-minute drop goal after a sustained assault on the English line. More Irish pressure would follow, with the English back row and especially Wilkinson required to produce big hit after big hit to resist the Irish onslaught.

Then came England's first try, a score of monumental importance that would rock Ireland back on their heels and

BELOW Ireland's Geordan Murphy cannot stop Mike Tindall from scoring a try described by the Irish as 'a stake through their heart'.

ABOVE Will Greenwood on his way to scoring two late tries.

provide a lead that the visitors would never relinquish. With the Irish scrum wheeling too far round in front of their own posts, Peter Stringer lost his footing and scooped up fresh air instead of the ball. Richard Hill was quick to seize this 8th-minute opportunity, grabbing the ball and passing to Matt Dawson, who weaved past two challenges before being pulled down a couple of yards from the line. There, in support, was Lawrence Dallaglio, who gleefully received Dawson's one-handed offload to dive in under the posts. The conversion was easy for Wilkinson. In the stands both Clive Woodward and Andy Robinson leapt to their feet in joy on the sight of Dallaglio's try. They knew how important it was to quell the early Irish fire. So, too, did Dallaglio. 'The force was with Ireland until then,' he admitted. 'We had

planned to put pressure on Stringer by attacking him at the base of the scrum to slow down the link between the Irish numbers nine and ten. The scrum twisted round, Richard picked up the ball and fed Matt and for a moment I thought he was going to score the try. Instead he put the try on a plate for me after Geordan Murphy had managed to stop him. I was in the right place at the right time. All I had to do was fall over the line. Yet the importance of the score was massive. We were playing into a strong wind so any points against Ireland were worth double. We also knew Ireland's objective was to get an early lead and stay out in front, gaining self-belief and increasing support from the crowd in the process. We knew that there was still plenty of work to be done, but the try put a big dent in Ireland's plans. That's why there was such a show of emotion. We'd been on the back foot until then, so to score any points, let alone a try under the posts, was exactly the boost we needed.'

Dawson explained how the Irish scrum-half faced a difficult choice when trying to save the try. 'At first I thought I was going to make it,' he said. 'Then in the corner of my eye I saw Peter Stringer racing across to cover. He knew that if he went high on me he'd run the risk of me fending him off to score, but if he went low he'd nail me but I'd stand a chance of offloading to Lawrence. He made the right decision in hitting me low because at least it guaranteed stopping me, and there was always the chance that either I'd get my pass wrong or Lawrence would drop the ball. Thankfully, we did neither.'

Back came Ireland as they launched attack after atack at the English line. They had the breeze behind their backs and knew a half-time lead was imperative. Geordan Murphy went desperately close to scoring, as did Kevin Maggs, the latter cut down by a trademark Wilkinson hit that was felt in the Lansdowne Road stands. Humphreys missed with a relatively simple penalty, then scored with a far harder chance from just inside the English half. Now there was one point in it as Ireland continued to press.

This was the key moment of the game. Ireland needed the lead as reward for their first-half dominance in terms of territory and possession. Instead, two Wilkinson drop goals, both with his weaker right foot, handed England a 13–6 half-time lead. 'The opportunities came my way so I took them,' Wilkinson said. 'We didn't care how we scored our points, as long as we scored. There's no doubt about it, though, we realised the psychological damage those drop goals could do. To have held them off and kept them out was already a big bonus for us. Then to go up the field and score six points to their none put us in excellent heart for the second half.'

He almost added a third five minutes into the second half, this time with a drop goal from much further out, but the touch judge disallowed it for a previous foul committed by England. The visitors' lead remained useful, but the destiny of the match, the Six Nations championship and the Grand Slam was by no means certain.

By this stage England had literally spilt blood for their cause. Richard Hill, Matt Dawson (twice), Graham Rowntree and Ben Kay had all required time out by the touchline for running repairs. The game was proving to be as tough as everyone had predicted.

Then, on the hour, it was Wilkinson's turn to leave the field, his injured shoulder being patched up and the inside of his mouth receiving seven stitches for a cut. While that was going on, Will Greenwood looked up and spun a short pass. Mike Tindall, who had adopted the perfect angle, collected the ball at pace, ran inside and past O'Driscoll, and set off on a scything twenty-five-metre burst towards the line. It looked like Geordan Murphy might stop the outside centre but instead he bounced off as Tindall dived over to score. It was, according to Eddie O'Sullivan, 'a stake through Irish hearts'. It also provided Paul Grayson with the opportunity to get his name on the scoresheet with a conversion before returning to the bench almost immediately as Wilkinson returned.

'It was the most important and the best try in my international career,' Tindall would say later. 'In the context of the game it was a massive try for England to score. At half-time I could see that the Irish came off the field wondering how on earth they were going to get past our defence. Then the try really disheartened them.

'I moved out and then came back in again ready to receive from Will Greenwood. Brian O'Driscoll, my opposite number, moved out with me, but didn't come back in again, leaving me the gap to exploit when I received from Will. Dennis Hickie came across and tried a tap tackle on me but missed, which left only Geordan Murphy to beat. The reason why he seemed to bounce off me was that he hit the ball with his body first. I would have been very upset if he'd stopped me. I'm really proud to have made such a contribution.'

At 20–6 with just a quarter of the game remaining it was looking increasingly like an English triumph, but Martin Johnson and his men were not going to leave anything to chance. Dallaglio was dragged down by Anthony Foley just short of Ireland's line, then Will Greenwood received Wilkinson's clever reverse pass and was steamrollered over by the English pack for the third English try of the afternoon. 'We planned to be very direct in our game because two years previously we got caught being too lateral,' Greenwood said. 'At first I thought I was going to score immediately, but Ronan O'Gara had just come on to the field and was fresh. As I hit him I thought I was going down on the floor but a second wave of pressure from the boys steaming in from behind saw me home.'

LEFT Greenwood's try in the corner presents
Wilkinson with a difficult chance.

Still refusing to accept the win was secure, Johnson asked Wilkinson to kick a penalty between the posts in the 71st minute to increase his side's lead to twenty-four points. 'Some people have enjoyed our failures over the past few years when it comes to Grand Slam games and we have learned from all this,' Wilkinson said. 'That's why we weren't going to throw any chance of scoring points. It was an example of how hard-nosed, ruthless and professional we've become. It's all been borne from previous experiences.'

At this juncture Will Greenwood turned to Josh Lewsey and asked him, 'Can you hear that?' Lewsey replied, 'I can't hear anything,' to which Greenwood responded, 'Exactly.' The noise of the Irish crowd had been well and truly silenced.

This was the first time in the whole game that Matt Dawson realised the extent of England's dominance. 'In such a game, when you have a split second to make a decision, a pass, a kick or a tackle, you don't have the luxury of letting your mind wander,' he said. 'I remember looking at the scoreboard for the first time when Jonny had that penalty kick at the posts. At the time the score read 27–6 and I remember being really surprised by the extent of our lead.'

As the game entered injury time, what had been for much of the time an intense battle turned into a late rout. First Greenwood scored his second try of the afternoon, intercepting Murphy's inside pass to run unopposed to the corner from twenty-five metres out. His salute to his father, watching from the stands, was well received. Dick Greenwood had been England's coach in the late 1980s when Grand Slams were seemingly unobtainable. 'Ireland were having to chase the game and my second try wouldn't have happened if the score was different,' said Greenwood, who, by scoring his third try of the Six Nations, finished joint top in the try-scorers' list for England with Josh Lewsey and Jason Robinson. For the previous two seasons Greenwood had enjoyed that honour on his own. 'They were thirty-odd points down with five minutes to go when Geordan tried to find Keith Gleeson. I couldn't believe my luck when the ball popped into my hands. I was smiling as I ran to the corner because I knew we'd won, the game was over and the Grand Slam was finally ours.'

Greenwood seemed to make a point of purposefully heading to the corner to touch down, resulting in a stiffer conversion chance for Jonny Wilkinson than it might have been. This prompted all kinds of speculation afterwards. 'There was nothing deep-rooted in it save for the fact that I was really enjoying the moment, especially after all the years

of lost opportunities, and I wanted to keep hold of the ball for as long as possible. As Jonny walked up to me to collect the ball for the conversion he muttered: "Thanks, pal, for that," but I noticed he was having a bit of fun too because he placed the ball right on the touch line to make the kick as hard as possible when he could have brought it in a yard or two.' Wilkinson recalled, 'It felt so good to look around and see smiles on the faces of all the England players while we were still playing. Five minutes before the kick-off the nerves and the anxiety made it almost unbearable to be out there. Now, five minutes before the end, the boot was on the other foot. I knew then that we'd won the Grand Slam.'

There was still time for Dan Luger to get in on the act. He had replaced Tindall for the last ten minutes and, in the sixth minute of injury time, he was on the receiving end of a flowing passage of passes initiated by Wilkinson's quickly taken tapped penalty, to score in the corner. Wilkinson's successful conversion proved to be the last kick of the game. For Luger, it was some compensation for a season that had been marred by injury, less than top form, and the severe trauma of losing his good friend Nick Duncombe. 'To come on and score the final try was a fantastic way personally to round off a Six Nations that I'll never forget, but mainly for the wrong reasons,' he explained. 'I'd been itching to get on to the field and what was the biggest boost was that when I did manage to get on I felt really happy and back to being my old self again, physically and especially mentally.'

Fittingly, Jason Leonard had supplied the final pass to Luger. 'Any Grand Slam is very precious,' the venerable prop said later. 'I should know because, although I've been fortunate to be involved in three previous Grand Slam-winning teams, I'd waited a long time for a fourth to come along. If I have to choose one emotion out of all the emotions I felt afterwards, I'd say it was relief; just huge relief.'

The celebrations were both joyous and respectful. Clive Woodward made a point of shaking the hand of each and every Irish player, mindful of the pain inflicted on the losing, Grand Slam-chasing side. Later he spoke of his relief and his pride in his team. 'Had we lost this game, the ramifications would have been huge,' he said, not for the first time during this championship. 'People would say this is a team that can't win the big games and there would have been justification for that. It would have been very tough to recover had we not nailed this one. If we'd lost, it would have been a very hard year going into the World Cup. We deliberately put the players under as much pressure as possible

and they responded with a colossal performance. I just can't say how good these guys are. They're the toughest guys I've been involved with both physically and mentally.'

Martin Johnson, who this time lifted the Six Nations trophy at Lansdowne Road under much happier circumstances, was just as relieved with the conclusion. 'We all knew we were under a lot of pressure to come through,' he said. 'We'd been too close too often but we've finally done it. If we had lost today it would have been horrible, a real nightmare. We came away against the form team in the championship and got a win.'

Lawrence Dallaglio, who experienced the pain of losing a Slam as captain back in 1999, had his say, too, after his most impressive performance of the tournament. 'This has been a long time coming,' he said. 'We've let people down in the past but we stood up when it counted. We deserved to win today. This was a huge day for English rugby. From a personal point of view I'd missed out on a Slam a few times and I knew this was my golden chance. It was a game that had to be won, not only from a team perspective, but from my own as well.'

Man-of-the-match Wilkinson, with fifteen points and the accolade of joint top tackler, also saw the significance of the day. 'We've taken a giant step forward, and I finally have something tangible to my name,' he stated, the blood still evident around his mouth. 'I can't tell you how good it feels finally to have a Grand Slam. This is the culmination of a lot of work. There's a lot of relief in there.'

Will Greenwood, after an unhappy few months both at home and at Harlequins, revealed how this time he knew the Slam would be England's. 'There was only one feeling on the bus: that the side was ready,' he said. 'Ready to do the business. I didn't think I played that well, but we've won the Grand Slam and I scored two tries. We've played prettier rugby and not won the Grand Slam. Maybe there's a lesson in that. This was very confrontational, very direct. What an effort by the forwards. Absolutely awesome. In the changing-room afterwards I shook hands with every one of them, from one to eight.

'We've been through some tough times as a squad in the past year. There's been some tough days, especially off the field, for a good number of the boys, myself included. We seem to have drawn a real inner strength from it all, though. That's why I just knew this time we'd get it right. This bunch of boys weren't going to let this one slip away. We weren't going to go so close again and fall at the final hurdle.'

An understandably delighted Matt Dawson said, 'It's been the best day in an England jersey for me, and one, I'm sure, that I will remember for the rest of my life. For the first time in this championship we went out and got the performance absolutely right. I have a mixture of satisfaction, of relief, of a feeling that we'd carried out our job to the best of our ability, and a feeling all round that this is why we play the game of rugby.'

Neil Back made a startling claim later that suggests a future career as a fortune-teller might be on the cards. 'Just for a split second in the changing-room moments before we were due to run out on to the pitch I sensed some self-doubt creeping into some of the boys,' he said. 'I announced that we were going to score forty points and that Ireland would not score more than six. I'd like to think Will Greenwood was helping me out by touching down the ball right in the corner for his second try,' Back added. 'Unfortunately, Jonny spoilt it for me by landing a really tough conversion from the other corner, which meant my prediction was two points out.

'Joking aside, I was pretty tearful afterwards. I tried to hide my emotions, but I knew how much winning the Grand Slam would mean to all of us, not just because of the past, but also for the future, with the World Cup beckoning. Our resolve has been absolute.'

Jason Robinson said, 'We knew it would be our day. There was a positive mood in the build-up and somehow it just felt right. We were convinced we wouldn't slip up this time. This was definitely one of the best achievements of my career. Winning all our autumn internationals and a Grand Slam sets us up well for the World Cup.'

Josh Lewsey was left scratching his head at how his rugby career had suddenly been turned upside down. At the start of the Six Nations he was no more than an England A player. By the end he had scored three tries in three appearances, and played his part in England's epic win in Dublin. 'In all honesty I couldn't see myself having any involvement in the Six Nations before it began,' he admitted. 'The key is to be ready and prepared for if the chance comes your way. If anyone had told me how my Six Nations would pan out I would have replied: "I'll have whatever you're having."'

All a disappointed Ireland could do was accept the inevitable. 'They strangled us up front and struck at critical moments,' conceded Eddie O'Sullivan. 'We had a very good second quarter against them and we needed to score at that time.' O'Driscoll commented: 'The number-one team in the world showed us why they are that today. The tempo was really fast, probably the quickest I've played in the Six Nations this year. We had scoring opportunities that we didn't take, and against England you can't do that.'

England had left their finest display in the 2003 Six Nations tournament until the last. In doing so they obliterated a very fine Irish team in Dublin, something that made the rest of the world of rugby sit up and take serious notice. More importantly, they finally had that elusive Grand Slam under their belts. With a June tour to New Zealand and Australia to look forward to, and the countdown to the World Cup including two warm-up internationals against France and one against Wales, it was crucial that they finally laid to rest the Slam hoodoo to build up their confidence.

On a Sunday night in Dublin, it looked to all the world that England had become very serious contenders for the World Cup.

ABOVE RIGHT Champions! The Holy Trinity: Messrs Hill, Back and Dallaglio, with the RBS Six Nations trophy.

ABOVE Richard Hill and Jonny Wilkinson enjoying a first Grand Slam.

CHAMPIONS 2003
The Royal Bank of Scotland

RBS 6 NATIONS

CHAMPION
The Royal Bank of Scotland

RIGHT the management team
with the Six Nations trophy:
top row (left to right):
Phil Keith-Roach, Assistant Coach;
Phil Pask, Physio;
Dave Reddin, Fitness Coach;
Richard Wegrzyk, Masseur.
Front row (left to right):
Andy Robinson, Coach;
Simon Hardy, Assistant Coach;
Tony Biscombe, Video Analyst;
Simon Kemp, Doctor;
Phil Larder, Assistant Coach;
Richard Prescott, Director of
Communications;
Dave Alred, Assistant Coach;
Barney Kenny, Physio;
Louise Ramsay, Manager;
Dave Tennison, Kitman;
Clive Woodward, Head Coach.

NEW ZEALAND 13
ENGLAND 15

Saturday, 14 June 2003 at Westpac Stadium, Wellington

NEW ZEALAND

Howlett, Rokococo (Muliaina, 72), Nonu, Umaga, Ralph, Spencer, Marshall (Devine, 48), Hewett, Oliver (Mealamu, 58), Somerville, Jack, Williams, Thorne, McCaw, So'oialo (Collins, 73)
SUBS (not used): Carter, Thorn, Hoeft

Try
Howlett

Conversion
Spencer

Penalties
Spencer 2

ENGLAND

Lewsey, Robinson, Greenwood, Tindall, Cohen, Wilkinson, Bracken, Rowntree, Thompson, Leonard (Vickery, 40), Johnson, Kay, Hill (J. Worsley, 72), Back, Dallaglio
SUBS (not used): West, Borthwick, Gomarsall, Grayson, Luger

Penalties
Wilkinson 4

Drop Goal
Wilkinson

Referee
Stuart Dickinson (Australia)

Attendance
38,450

CHAPTER NINE

'To come down to Wellington and beat the All Blacks is awesome'

The professional rugby life dictates that there is little time to savour the joys of success, even when that success is as monumental as a first Grand Slam in eight years. And so it was for Clive Woodward's men at the tail-end of a remarkable season. For the Northampton and Gloucester contingent – players such as Matt Dawson, Ben Cohen, Steve Thompson, James Simpson-Daniel, Andy Gomarsall and Trevor Woodman – there was the small matter of the Powergen Cup Final. For the Leicester Tigers a Heineken Cup quarter-final against Munster beckoned, a game that would give the Irish some consolation, and Martin Johnson and Neil Back a fair bit of misery. And for everyone else there was either the chase for the top three and the play-offs in the Zurich Premiership or the battle to avoid relegation that went down to the wire.

ABOVE Martin Johnson back in his beloved New Zealand.

As late as the weekend prior to Clive Woodward's selection of his main squad for the short but vital June tour Down Under, key players were featuring in key games that would play a part in the management's decision-making. At Twickenham, a young-looking England fifteen was well-beaten by an experienced Barbarians team, although the Newcastle centre Jamie Noon was impressive. Wasps, who would go on to clinch the league title by beating Gloucester in the Grand Final, had already claimed the Parker Pen Cup, seeing off Bath at Reading's Madejski Stadium with ease. In the process Danny Grewcock, Bath's captain and a man who should have been pushing Ben Kay hard for the second-row spot alongside Martin Johnson, was sent off for punching Lawrence Dallaglio. A disciplinary hearing held after the game decided to mete out a fourteen-day ban to Grewcock, which meant he would miss both games on the New Zealand leg of the tour, against the Maoris and the All Blacks.

Initially Woodward nevertheless named Grewcock in his tour party on the understanding that the Bath lock would appeal. 'I don't see Danny as a liability,' he insisted. 'I see him as one of the world's best players. I wouldn't play anyone in the team whom I didn't think could control himself under the utmost pressure.' Bath, however, decided against appealing because of both the logistical problems of European Rugby Cup Ltd holding a tribunal before England's departure for New Zealand and the risk that a rejected appeal could result in a longer sentence.

So, two days after first naming his squad, Woodward omitted Grewcock. 'Danny and I spoke at length and have agreed that it's in our best interests that he stays in England for the duration of the tour,' explained the England Head Coach. 'However, Danny will be joining the squad when it reconvenes in late July and he remains an important part of our plans as we prepare for the World Cup.'

Injuries had deprived Woodward of half a dozen likely tourists. Charlie Hodgson, Austin Healey, Lewis Moody,

Julian White, Alex Sanderson and the young back-row forward James Forrester may well have been on the long flight to the Southern Hemisphere. However, a strong-looking squad of thirty-seven was announced at the Pennyhill Park Hotel in Bagshot for the three games against the Maoris, New Zealand and Australia. Although some interesting choices were made with a view to the Maoris game and as back-up to the main squad – players such as the Wasps centre Stuart Abbott, his back-row club colleague Paul Volley and the Gloucester flanker Andy Hazell were the three uncapped names to be selected – the squad that demolished Ireland to clinch the Grand Slam was there in force.

Woodward, who was at the end of his first season as Head Coach when England were last in New Zealand, considered the forthcoming test matches to be so important that he simply refused to wrap his star players in cotton-wool before the World Cup. 'What happened five years ago was a very low point in the history of the game,' he explained. 'It was a total mismatch and I was determined it would not happen again. It's no good New Zealand and Australia bringing full-strength teams here if we don't do the same when we go there. There are risks involved, but this is the right thing to do. We're prepared to put everything on the line. If your mindset is to be worried about losing, then you might as well not play test-match rugby. I've not even thought about the possibility of losing. I see this trip simply as a huge opportunity. It's been a long season, but the senior players are not shirking it. They are very excited at the challenge of getting something out of the tour and then having a good break.'

The big names had something to say, too, about the mouth-watering test matches awaiting them in Wellington and Melbourne. Martin Johnson, a confirmed admirer of New Zealand rugby after his eighteen-month sabbatical back in 1989–90, was particularly looking forward to returning to the North Island. 'New Zealand will be very keen to welcome us to Wellington,' he said. 'It's been a long time since they've seen our full-strength test side. They appreciate that we're serious contenders these days and they'll be wanting to make an impact on us, that's for sure. They still see themselves as the best in the world. There's no question that for us to win we're going to have to play to our absolute maximum.

'Let's be honest about it, they lost by only three points at our stadium at the end of their long season. They had big names missing but still beat us on the try count by three to one. We have the Grand Slam, which is a huge weight off our shoulders, and we're all very hungry to prove to the world that we can win in places like Wellington. If we're close to our best, we can win. If we're not, we'll be taught a harsh lesson.'

Jonny Wilkinson explained how the 1998 Tour of Hell, in which an under-strength England were beaten 64–22 and 40–10 by New Zealand, and 76–0 by Australia, was the making of him. 'I didn't enjoy it, but it has been hugely beneficial for me,' he said. 'The experience made it possible for me to speed up my improvement. Going through such an intense range of emotions allowed me to progress quicker than I would have otherwise. In terms of my education, it was vital. It made me realise that there can never be any room for getting carried away. I thought I was getting somewhere in the game until I went on that tour. It was as if someone were saying to me: "You think you've done well, but hold on. You've got a long way to go even to get close to this level." I knew I would have to work harder if I was ever to get to that level. I raised my standard and set out to reach a level which I would be satisfied with. In one respect I've been distancing myself from the experience, but I have always maintained that it taught me more than anything else I have gone through, or ever will. When I came back from that trip I knew I couldn't afford to let it be my last. I've had the chance to go back to Australia a few times, but never to New Zealand, until now. I am very honoured I have the chance to go back and it would be nice now to do it a little differently from the last time.'

On the other side of the world, the New Zealand coach, John Mitchell, was naming his squad for the forthcoming test matches against England, Wales and France. True to form, Mitchell kept to his tradition of ignoring reputations. The biggest name to discover he no longer figured in Mitchell's plans was stand-off Andrew Mehrtens, who, with 932 points from 66 tests, is the third-highest scorer in test-match history. Mehrtens has often spoken in the past of how much he enjoys beating the English, accusing them of being gloating, poor winners. Yet now he was not considered good enough even to sit on the bench.

'We know what Mehrtens can offer,' said Mitchell. 'There are a couple of areas to his game which we'd like him to improve, but, just as with all the others who have missed out, the door is not closed.' Carlos Spencer, the guiding light behind Auckland's successful retention of the Super 12 title, was preferred in the pivotal position.

ABOVE Lawrence Dallaglio powers his way through the All Black defence.

With Jonah Lomu's chronic kidney condition now so bad that dialysis was expected to be the next step in his long medical battle, the big winger and scourge of England was not only ruled out of the Wellington test match but faced the likely prospect of missing the World Cup and being forced to retire from the game. Lomu's absence was no great surprise, but the omission of full-back Christian Cullen most certainly was. The man with the best strike rate in international rugby – 46 tries from just 57 tests – learned that his past exploits were not enough to save him from the drop. Mitchell decided to select just the one specialist full-back, Leon MacDonald, making it possible to include Auckland's two uncapped wings, the colourfully named Joe Rokococo and Mils Muliaina. Back-row forward Reuben Thorne was reinstated as captain, which meant his predecessor the previous November at Twicken-

ham, Taine Randell, was surplus to requirements.

Before having to face the All Blacks, Woodward had the small matter of having to deal with the New Zealand Maoris in a game played at the 23,000-seater Yarrow Park Stadium in New Plymouth, halfway up the western coast of the North Island. This would, to all intents and purposes, be played with the same intensity as a test match. The Maoris, boasting both Randell and Cullen, are usually every touring team's nightmare. Until 2001, when they lost to a full Wallaby side, they had been unbeaten for twenty-four games over seven years, with victories over twelve international teams, including a 62–14 thrashing of England in 1998 at Rotorua.

While the core of the England test team was left behind in Wellington to prepare for the All Blacks game five days later, twenty-two players made the short flight to New Plymouth fully aware that a place on the bench in the test, at least, was up for grabs, as well as the chance to stake a claim for the World Cup squad. In particular this was the opportunity for Phil Vickery, named as captain, to prove he was returning to top form after the back problems that had kept him out of the Six Nations.

In windy, rainy conditions, England came through in some style, winning 9–23 and inflicting a first defeat on home soil for ten years in the process. Even though they were playing into the teeth of the filthy elements, they held a 6–10 interval lead thanks to a Simon Shaw try from a maul, converted by Paul Grayson, and a Grayson penalty. Andy Gomarsall then added a second-half try, and, with Grayson succeeding with the resulting conversion as well as two further penalties, England were home, if not exactly dry.

Despite this being only a tour game, Woodward believed it would have a huge bearing on the probable test side watching back in Wellington on television. 'Martin Johnson and the boys will take a lot out of that,' he said. 'There will be a spring in their step at training tomorrow and it really sets up the test week.' He would, in particular, have taken note of Joe Worsley's display, plus that of lock Steve Borthwick and fly-half Grayson, who, in testing conditions, put boot to ball with conclusive results.

Indeed, these three were all rewarded with call-ups to the reserves when Woodward named his twenty-two for the New Zealand test the following morning. Phil Vickery was also on the bench, as was hooker Dorian West, not far off thirty-six years of age, who nudged Mark Regan out of the reserve number-two spot. Despite Gomarsall's impressive cameo against the Maoris, Kyran Bracken was preferred as back-up to Matt Dawson.

Naming the starting fifteen was, for once, both a comparatively simple task for Woodward and one that did not spring any surprises. After seeing how they demolished Ireland in Dublin to claim the Grand Slam in their previous test match, Woodward rightly decided he had to stick with the same tried and tested group of players. 'Those who beat the Maoris were outstanding and put a lot of pressure on the twenty-two places for the test team,' Woodward explained. 'But I was determined to play a settled side.'

By contrast, John Mitchell, in announcing his test squad the same day, threw up a number of names new to England as he plumped for youth, form, flair and potential. Top of the pile was the selection of the Fijian flyer Joe Rokococo, who, having just turned twenty, would become the youngest player to be capped by the All Blacks since a nineteen-year-old Lomu made his debut in 1994. Born in Nadi but moving to Auckland at the age of five, Rokococo had first made his mark two years before when he hit the English Schools with a hat-trick while playing for New Zealand Schools in Dunedin. A year later he scored twenty-seven tries in half a dozen sevens tournaments before a broken ankle ruled him out of the Commonwealth Games.

Although at six feet three and fifteen stones he is a big man, what really sets Rokococo apart from his closest rivals is his pace. Those who feel Doug Howlett is like lightning may be shocked to discover that Rokococo is even faster, with a time of 4.66 seconds over 40 metres. 'Howlett's sharp, but not as sharp as Joe,' said New Zealand's backs coach, Robbie Deans. 'He's a very level-headed kid and a fast learner. We believe these guys can cope with the cauldron we're putting them in and there's nothing for him to be afraid of.' The second new cap, Ma'a Nonu, just twenty-one years of age, also made the breakthrough after a successful Super 12. Howlett was restored to full-back following the withdrawal of Leon MacDonald. The unfortunate MacDonald had endured a worrying number of head injuries over the previous year and was still complaining of headaches. In total, Mitchell retained just four of the experimental team who outscored England 4–3 on tries but ultimately lost to them at Twickenham.

Former All Blacks captain and hooker Anton Oliver was recalled after a year dogged by injury. His previous thirty-nine caps accounted for nearly a third of the pack's test-match experience, and coach Mitchell understood the importance of winning the battle up front against an set of English forwards boasting 422 caps between them. 'Guys such as Martin Johnson and Lawrence Dallaglio understand what test rugby is all about,' he conceded. 'They carry the ball well, too, and they like to put huge dents in the advantage line.'

Mitchell, whose two and a half years as Woodward's assistant coach with England made him better qualified than most to view the opposition, was a clear admirer, too, of the systems being introduced by defensive coach Phil Larder. 'They're very well organised defensively and the heart of the team comes from that organisation,' said

Mitchell. 'They were clearly the best side in the Six Nations. Any side that concedes only 9.2 points a game there has to be considered as a very well-organised and structured side. Their line speed is outstanding and they're very effective in the tackle.'

Although Mitchell and his All Blacks may have been full

Post added: 'Their limited, league-style brand of rugby gives a new meaning to the phrase low-risk. Anything more grandiose will show up their lack of speed across the paddock, the frailty of their backs, and would expose them to attacks from turnovers. It seems highly unlikely that such dour rugby will have success at the World Cup.' Such com-

of respect for England, others Down Under were not. The Wales coach, Kiwi Steve Hansen, went public in saying that New Zealand 'would be too good' for the English. The local media went a great deal further. 'It's time to bring the Poms down a peg or two,' read one headline in a Sunday newspaper. Even after the comfortable win over the Maoris the response was hardly kind. 'On a dry ground it's unlikely England will have the skill or the pace to match the All Blacks,' said the *Daily News*, while the *Dominion*

ABOVE Captain Johnson dishes out
the orders while Wilkinson looks on.

ABOVE RIGHT Johnson leading by example.

ments would surely only fuel England's determination to secure their second test victory on New Zealand soil, their first having been back in 1973, before many of the current crop of England players had even been born.

However, the loss of scrum-half Matt Dawson on the Wednesday before the match was undoubtedly a blow.

it.' His replacement, Kyran Bracken, made the jump up into the starting fifteen while Andy Gomarsall took his place on the bench. Bracken was quick to remind his opponents of history repeating itself. 'The last time this happened to me was also against New Zealand in 1993 when Dewi Morris pulled out on the Thursday before the game,'

Once again his troublesome thigh let him down during a fitness test. 'I thought Matt would make it, which is why I named him in the side on Tuesday,' explained Woodward. 'It won't affect how we play. Sometimes you get a better performance from someone given an unexpected chance.' Dawson himself was understandably downbeat: 'This is a long way to come for physio,' he complained. 'This has come as a real shock to me as I hadn't even contemplated not being available for this game. I really thought I'd make

he recalled. 'I came in for my England debut and we won. I'm hoping this is a good omen.'

The rest of the England team, meanwhile, were having to defend themselves against continuing accusations from the New Zealand media and former players, notably Wallaby great David Campese, that they lacked any style or finesse. 'Their perception of us is that we are very much a forward-orientated team and that we don't have any backs,' said Lawrence Dallaglio. 'They portray us as a team who like to kick the ball up in the air and are only happy playing in wet conditions. How they can say that when you have the likes of Jason Robinson, Ben Cohen, Will Greenwood, Jonny Wilkinson and others in your team beats me. Nothing could be further from the truth. In eight tests this season we've scored thirty tries.' Dallaglio's first visit to New Zealand was proving to be an eye-opener. 'It's the missing piece in the jigsaw puzzle,' he added. 'You can go about your business as a rugby player back home and no one bothers you. Here, you are in the eye of the storm.'

Wilkinson, meanwhile, dismissed Campese's claims that he would be targeted in the hope of putting him out of the World Cup. 'I have to play my normal game,' he explained. 'I can't worry about what may or may not happen. If they target me then it means they are not looking at someone else. That will be to our advantage.'

His opposite number, All Black stand-off Carlos Spencer, would be given the utmost respect from England, however. Phil Larder made it clear what a threat he could be. 'I went to watch him play for Auckland when I was the Great Britain rugby league coach,' said Larder. 'I wanted to persuade him to switch codes. He scored four tries that day. I have massive admiration for him. He's one of the most dangerous running footballers in the world. He has so much vision, great hands and zippy acceleration. Trying to cope with him and those around him is as challenging a prospect as I've had. But defence is all about pressure, and that can be applied in many ways.'

Over in the All Black camp, open-side flanker Richie McCaw was preparing himself for an almighty battle between the packs. 'We know they are strong up front,' he conceded. 'But if we do what we want to do, they can't do what they want to do. How many sides have taken them on up front? You have to match them there, take them on. It will be tough, and if it is to happen, it may not be until late in the game. But you have to get at least parity because, if you don't, you will come second, that's for sure. We believe we can match them.' His captain, Reuben Thorne, confessed that there could have been an easier opening to the Southern Hemisphere's winter season of internationals. 'This is a tough one to start with,' the back-row forward said. 'We have been thrown in at the deep end.'

Lock forward Ali Williams, meanwhile, revealed a gesture made by Martin Johnson after England's narrow win back in November at Twickenham. 'Martin came into our changing room at the end and I thought he wanted my shirt,' he said. 'I explained that I wanted to keep it because it might be the only one I get, but he gave me his, saying: "This is yours. I really admired the way you played."' On the eve of the test Woodward spoke of how all the criticism levelled at his men during the week was like water off a duck's back. 'I don't care how we are seen down here,' he insisted. 'We're the most unpopular side wherever we go – Ireland, Wales, Scotland, France – so you just get used to it and get on with it. In fact, you almost thrive on it. I wasn't unhappy about what's been written and said. I was just amused after trying to play rugby in a monsoon against the Maoris and winning well to be told that we should have been chucking the ball around. Actually, we probably chucked the ball about too much. Some New Zealanders have this impression of English rugby that we all play in Wellington boots and in grass that is two feet long. The public here think that England are going to get smashed, which could make for an interesting night. You never beat the All Blacks, you just score more points than them. This team doesn't try to wind up anybody and is way beyond getting wound up by things in the media. We're just concerned about the game. Everyone's got to step up or we won't win. We are going to have to play better than we did against Ireland because this team is a significant step above anything we've played in the Six Nations. If we're really serious about the World Cup in October, then it's important that we front up here and perform. We want to look the All Blacks in the eye and take them on.'

By the Saturday night Wellington's customary winter gales were whipping up again inside the 'Cake Tin', the nickname given to the Westpac Stadium by locals due to its enclosed, circular shape. With rain falling steadily, too, conditions would prove to be difficult. They would determine the way this game would be played, but not the achievement by the England team which recorded a historic victory in what is arguably the toughest venue in the game. With just four months to go to the start of the World Cup in Australia, Woodward's men had scored a massive psychological blow, as much in the manner of the win as in the result itself.

So England's amazing twelve-month countdown to the World Cup continued at breakneck speed, with each new feat seeming to outstrip the last. If beating all three Southern Hemisphere giants at Twickenham in back-to-back tests, then capturing a long-overdue Grand Slam with the

ABOVE Tension cracks within the forward ranks.

most emphatic of wins in Dublin were not enough, they had now defeated New Zealand in their own backyard. The result made it a record-breaking twelve successive test-match wins for England and an incredible twenty-sixth victory in their past twenty-eight tests, the kind of form that undoubtedly wins World Cups.

For a team supposedly unable to travel, and roundly written off in New Zealand by an expectant Kiwi media and public, the performance England gave silenced the crowd long before the end of what was a far from pretty but utterly compelling meeting between the two countries most fancied to meet in November's World Cup Final.

Although England's squad were heroes to a man, especially captain Johnson and his trusty lieutenant Dallaglio, Jonny Wilkinson's impeccable place-kicking in terribly testing conditions, in contrast to opposite stand-off Carlos Spencer's

decidedly ordinary display with the boot, ultimately made the difference. Wilkinson's drop goal just past the hour pulled England into a nine-point lead, and, although a Howlett try and a Spencer conversion meant that the last eighteen minutes were tense, it was enough to see England home.

Yet the main reasons why the slight pre-match under-dogs emerged triumphant were their defence and a spirit highlighted by a ten-minute spell just after the break which proved to be the turning point of the game. Stuart Dickinson, the Australian referee who would be on the receiving end afterwards of universal criticism for the way in which he constantly penalised both teams, had already warned the England back row about repeated infringements around the base of the ruck. So it was no great surprise when, in the 46th minute, he sent Neil Back to the sin bin. Just sixty seconds later, the otherwise impressive Lawrence Dallaglio followed Back off – for the same offence, interfering with the ball – and the signs were ominous. From the resulting penalty New Zealand, who had begun the game with a

ABOVE Wilkinson prepares to spin the ball wide.

bigger, heavier pack, understandably declined the kick at goal and opted for a scrum underneath the English posts. The assumption, of course, was that there was no way the depleted England pack could resist, and the inevitable result would be a try and a simple conversion. However, four times the All Blacks eight packed down against the England six, and on all four occasions they were rebuffed. Rodney So'oialo believed he might have scrambled over for a try, only for the Australian video referee, Peter Marshall, to judge that the dreadlocked number eight had grounded before the line and then employed a double movement to make it over. To make matters worse for the home side, seconds before a pumped-up Back returned to the fray, Wilkinson slotted home his fourth penalty out of four attempts, which gave England an astonishing three-point advantage from their thirteen-man spell. For the All Blacks, this must have been soul-destroying.

'When our six men faced the eight from New Zealand underneath our own posts, I told our remaining forwards that we had to give it our all,' Johnson explained later. 'We just had to go for it. The pressure was huge. We couldn't bring a back into the forwards because that would have given them a huge amount of space to work in. If they had scored a try it would have been seven points that would have ultimately won the match for the All Blacks. Instead we held firm and I'd like to pay special tribute to the front row for leading the way in holding off an opposition pack with a huge advantage. You could see what a blow it was to New Zealand in failing to score, and then to concede three further points as Jonny's boot inflicted the damage must have made it doubly worse for them.' When he was asked

ABOVE Ben Cohen evades Justin Marshall's grip.

what else went through his mind at this point, he replied: 'Almost my spine.'

'They fancied their chances all right,' said prop Graham Rowntree, who was in the front line of the under-strength England pack. 'What they were saying just fired us up. Adversity pulls the best out of some people. It sounds crazy after you've just lost two forwards, but I wasn't too worried because we were scrummaging so well. We all geed each other up to keep them out. Sheer determination, that's what got us through. I've never been in a position like that before and I never want to be again. Nobody else would have fancied our chances, but we did. We lived to tell the tale.'

Neil Back, having witnessed the heroics from the touchline, described his mood as he returned to the pitch. 'I was as determined as I've ever been to play my part,' he said. 'What the England pack achieved without both myself and Lawrence was incredible, and it really motivated me when I got back on. I obviously felt disappointed to have dropped England in it a bit, but I also felt relieved to see how they held out, and I was also inspired.'

Eventually New Zealand's frustration boiled over when lock Ali Williams repeatedly stamped on Josh Lewsey's head with five minutes remaining as the full back lay beneath a pile of bodies in a ruck. As Lewsey was nowhere near the ball, England were rightly incensed, as indeed seemed the authorities. Shortly after the game had finished, the independent citing commissioner, Australian Michael Somes, cited Williams. His fate would be decided the following morning.

England had made the best possible start when Wilkinson grabbed a first-minute lead with a penalty made to look simple in spite of the swirling wind and rain. Spencer hit back after ten minutes with a penalty. A little later Lewsey bundled All Black wing Caleb Ralph out of play by the corner flag with a try-saving tackle. A second Wilkinson penalty, this time from the touchline, eased England ahead again, before Spencer drew the scores level four minutes before half-time.

After the break Phil Vickery replaced Jason Leonard and immediately brought power and urgency to England's loose play. Another Wilkinson penalty, again from a difficult angle, regained the lead for England early in the second half and, after his fourth penalty, he rounded off his performance with his 61st-minute drop goal from close range.

At this point it seemed game over, but New Zealand made a fight of it with a try that should never have been allowed. Spotting a hole at the back of the English defence after Lewsey had ventured forward, Spencer punted the ball downfield and watched as Howlett raced past a retreating Dallaglio in the chase for the ball to touch down first. Replays, however, revealed quite clearly how both Howlett and Ralph were offside as Spencer kicked. No matter. Although Spencer converted, he then missed his fourth kick out of seven attempts three minutes later.

It would prove to be New Zealand's last chance as England held on to win. As Johnson trudged off the pitch he told his club and second-row colleague Ben Kay: 'This is the sort of thing you can sit in your chair and look back on when you are an old man.'

Afterwards Clive Woodward almost burst with pride as he spoke of this tremendous test victory. In summing up his fabulous England team the Head Coach chose four words: 'Guts, determination, heroics, magnificent,' he said, before looking ahead to the World Cup. 'You don't get to become the number-one-ranked team in the world, win twelve back-to-back test matches and beat New Zealand twice in a row without being special. We're going to be a lot better, too, by the World Cup. If we meet New Zealand again in that competition we'll be very confident we can win, now that we've beaten them twice in succession. This game was all about winning, and the result was all that mattered.'

On having to marshal thirteen men against fifteen, Woodward made an interesting point. 'We often practise with fourteen players in case of one yellow card, but never with thirteen,' he admitted. 'It doesn't come down to luck.

It comes down to everyone thinking and acting correctly under severe pressure. The sheer will to win was there in abundance. You can't put a price on that. It's something which has been created over a long period of time.'

Phil Larder backed up these comments, with special ref-

erence to his captain. 'Johnno is an extraordinary player who will be talked about for many years to come,' he said. 'He keeps his head when others are losing theirs. But he's also helped by others who possess great leadership qualities. These guys have so much heart and so much belief. They

ABOVE Phil Vickery has an inspired second half in Wellington.

have this special something. I don't know what you call it, something that comes from deep within. It's a desire to succeed. It comes from the environment which Clive has built.'

John Mitchell was magnanimous in defeat and paid tribute to the form team in world rugby, suggesting that this result would reverberate all the way to the World Cup. 'Psychologically, this was a fantastic win for England,' he said. 'They are rightly considered to be the number-one side in the world, they would have gained a great deal from this mentally and they will proceed to play Australia next week and on to the World Cup in October with renewed confidence.'

His vice-captain, Tana Umaga, was full of respect, too. 'The people in New Zealand should respect them for what they have done,' he said afterwards. 'It's what teams do that counts, not what they say, and these guys are doing it all. They have that cohesive unit throughout, and it doesn't matter where they play. They have something which travels the world with them. They are what we're striving to be. They're going to take some stopping at the World Cup. They know their game plan, they all believe in it and put it into operation. Their defence was one of the best I've ever

ABOVE It's over! England win for only the second time on New Zealand turf.

seen. They've beaten us twice in a row and they operate like a club side, playing week in, week out.'

As the England players emerged from the dressing-room they were exhausted but ecstatic with the result. 'To come down to Wellington and beat the All Blacks is awesome,' said Wilkinson. 'Our last big away win was against South Africa in Bloemfontein back in 2000, but this rates even higher. It was hard fought and very direct, but we did what we had to do.' Wing Ben Cohen described the scene in the England dressing-room: 'It was like a battlefield,' he said. 'There were bodies all over the place. We're very happy, but also extremely tired. We'll take a win in Wellington any day.' Scrum-half Bracken added, 'It's one of the best wins I've ever been involved in,' while Josh Lewsey said, 'We didn't even play that well, so it bodes very well for us. I've got a few stamps in the face and on the back of the head, but I'll take that for a win in New Zealand.'

Richard Hill, the only member of the England back row

left on the field during that crucial ten-minute period, said, 'My two colleagues in the back row decided to desert me. Still, I thought the back row during that period of time was awesome. Joking apart, it was a huge effort from the remaining six men, especially the front three. It was backs-to-the-wall stuff, but we came through and will be better for the experience.'

Steve Thompson, the young hooker who has made such an impact in just a couple of years with England, took time to pay tribute to the older members of the pack, written off in some quarters for being too old. 'They're just extraordinary,' said the Northampton man. 'With them you can't talk about age – Johnson, Dallaglio, Back, Hill, Leonard. For me it's an absolute honour, a massive highlight of my career, to be playing alongside them. The old saying goes if you're good enough, you're old enough, but they show it's the other way round, too: if you're good enough, you're young enough.'

Jason Robinson, too, was proud of his and his team's achievement. 'Nobody can ever accuse us of choking again when the chips are down,' he said. 'Victories over New Zealand are to be treasured because I know to my cost how hard they are to come by. There's an immense satisfaction of a rare win in a place where English teams hardly ever succeed. That said, we know we didn't play near to our best, and yet, at the same time, we have done something that no English team has done for thirty years and we did it despite going down to thirteen men at one stage. This has proved beyond doubt that we can win the big games away. None of us will ever forget the night we beat the All Blacks in New Zealand.'

Martin Johnson best summed up his and his team's emotions. 'This success has massive implications,' he said. 'To win for only the second time ever on their soil is an immense achievement. It's as big a win as I can recall playing in in an England shirt. As I went around the dressing-room afterwards I could see a side who were drained, and players who had given their all, but I was proud of every single one of them. The first thing I said when we got back to the dressing-room was how important a result this was, not only for the players, but for English rugby as a whole.

'It wasn't too long ago that we were losing close encounters against the top teams. Now we're winning them, and this is not down to luck or coincidence, but to hard work borne out of our success in the past couple of years. All of us wanted to come down to New Zealand, face the All Blacks,

and win. For the likes of myself and Lawrence, it would be a first time ever for England in New Zealand. For others, such as Jonny, it was a chance to make amends for those heavy defeats back in 1998. And for everyone, after the Grand Slam, it was a chance to assess ourselves against the very best. I think we've proved beyond any doubt that we are now a team on top of our game and to be reckoned with.'

Indeed England had proved that, but the current world champions were waiting in Melbourne to give them their next text. However, for once England would enter the game confident of victory, for the first time ever on Australian soil.

ABOVE A weary Wilkinson leaves the field at the Westpac.

AUSTRALIA 14

ENGLAND 25

Saturday, 21 June 2003 at the Telstra Dome, Melbourne

AUSTRALIA

Latham, Sailor, Turinui (Rogers 59), S. Kefu, Roff, Grey (Tuqiri 64), Gregan, Young, Paul (Cannon 52), Noriega (Darwin 64), Giffin, Sharpe (Vickerman 44), Lyons, Waugh, T. Kefu

Subs (not used): Heenan, Whitaker

Try

Sailor

Pens

Roff 3

ENGLAND

Lewsey, Robinson, Greenwood, Tindall, Cohen, Wilkinson, Bracken (Dawson 52), Woodman, Thompson, Vickery, Johnson, Kay (Borthwick 63-68), Hill (J. Worsley 52), Back, Dallaglio

Subs (not used): Regan, Leonard, Luger, King

Tries

Greenwood, Tindall, Cohen

Penalties

Wilkinson 2

Conversions

Wilkinson 2

Attendance

54,000

Referee

David McHugh (Ireland)

CHAPTER TEN

'Beating Australia is special, but then again we're a special team'

There was no time to savour the epic win in Wellington. On the Sunday afternoon, less than twenty-four hours after winning at the Westpac, England were leaving New Zealand and flying to Melbourne for their encounter six days later with the world champions. However, just a day after beating the All Blacks, more controversy flared up, this time concerning the fate of the New Zealand lock, Ali Williams.

After he had stamped on Josh Lewsey late in the second half, Williams had been charged by an independent citing commissioner, Michael Somes, after TV cameras had revealed the full horror of his actions. The judicial panel, having met on the Sunday morning for ninety minutes, then ruled after viewing the video replays that the evidence was inconclusive and left it at that. According to the panel, contact was 'inadvertent and incidental'. Clive Woodward was understandably furious on hearing the news.

'If it had been an England player, we'd still be in Wellington now and probably all be locked up,' he said. 'Williams has got off scot free, which is just wrong in my opinion. There is a feeling among the players that it is one rule for everyone else and one rule for the English. Sitting at home is Danny Grewcock, who threw a few punches at Lawrence Dallaglio in a club game, which isn't going to hurt anybody. He doesn't make the trip, is banned for two matches, but a guy stamps on someone's head – and the cuts on Lewsey's head are bad – and gets off with no explanation. We would be a lot happier if we had an explanation as to why it was not a punishable offence. For him to get nothing is poor. We are not happy as a group of players about this.' Recalling the Twickenham battle against South Africa the previous November, Woodward said, 'In two games running now we've played Southern Hemisphere teams where there's been stuff going on. There's a lot at stake and people have got to control themselves.'

Josh Lewsey, with three stitches in the back of his head, added, 'If it's intentional, then something needs to be done about it. The ball was a long, long way away from where I was. If that was in the Northern Hemisphere, then someone would have to bear the consequences of it.'

To make matters worse, England departed from Wellington with a lot of negative reaction from the locals to the manner of their victory. One newspaper went as far as to describe the England players as 'Orcs on steroids', a reference borrowed from *The Lord of the Rings* trilogy of films shot on location in New Zealand, and a description that provoked a mixed reaction of amusement and bemusement in the English camp. There would be a great deal more nonsense to come in the following five days as well, before the meeting with the Wallabies.

Indeed, barely had they set foot in Australia than Reuben Thorne, the All Black captain, was publicly stat-

ing that England would lose to the Wallabies. He conveniently ignored the conditions in Wellington and concluded that England's approach was negative and defence-orientated. 'It will be a real shame if England's ball-killing tactics continue through to the World Cup because it's not positive, teams just shutting each other down,' he said. 'Australia will certainly match them in the

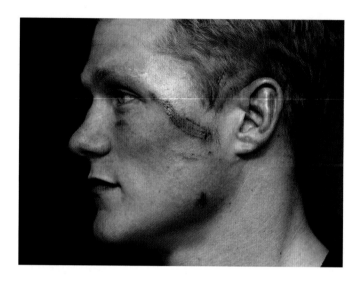

ABOVE The scars of battle: Josh Lewsey, the morning after his face met up with Ali Williams's studs.

set-pieces, and then it's just up to what you do with the ball in hand. If I had to pick it, I'd say Australia will win.' This was just the start of some useful motivation that would come England's way that week.

Martin Johnson put the record straight early in the week. Labelling his Southern Hemisphere critics 'naïve', he went on to say: 'I think they have a few perceived ideas of what our rugby and what our players are about that are wrong. They think we are still a forward-dominated, ten-man rugby team, which is certainly not the case. You have to deal with what you face on the day, both conditions-wise and opposition-wise. Saturday against Australia will be totally different. It will be fast and hard and dry, and there will be no wind. If the opportunity is there, we'll move the ball. We have good wingers and a good back line, but we need to get some decent ball for them to use.'

Australia, in the meantime, had warmed up for the England clash with two comfortable wins over Ireland and Wales. The Irish, having lost out on the Grand Slam to England in a heavy home defeat, were beaten by another World Cup contender in Perth, 45–16, after a

ABOVE Will Greenwood ends a magnificent fourteen-phase move to score England's first try against Australia.

second-half thumping. Despite this they came out of the game believing England were still a step ahead of their Southern Hemisphere opponents. 'Provided they are at full strength, I think they will be too good for Australia,' said the Irish acting captain, David Humphreys. Wales, meanwhile, shortly after England had seen off the All Blacks, fared surprisingly better, limiting Australia to a 30–10 win in Sydney and exposing some Wallaby deficiencies in the process.

Afterwards, there were far bigger problems with the news that the Australian stand-off, Elton Flatley, who had scored two tries at Twickenham the previous November, and had shone against both the Irish and the Welsh, had been sent home to Brisbane by Wallaby coach Eddie Jones. Flatley had been conspicuous by his absence at a recovery session on the Sunday morning, having celebrated with friends in Sydney till the early hours. It would mean that he would miss the England test, which, considering that Australia were already lacking their first-choice stand-off, the injured Stephen Larkham, provided quite a dilemma for Jones. He would be choosing between centre Nathan Grey and wing Joe Roff as a replacement.

'I've definitely let myself down a bit,' a repentant Flatley said. 'It is a tough lesson to learn. I went out with a few friends and missed the team meeting. The Wallabies have a strict code of conduct. You've got to be there and I wasn't. I let the team down as well.' Jones revealed that Flatley had received a prior warning for a similar breach

during the Tri-Nations series the previous year. 'It was a tough decision,' he said. 'Elton is a good young fellow. Unfortunately, he stepped out of line and he has to face the consequences. Discipline is more important than worrying about short-term results. It was out of character for him.'

No such problems for England, however, although Clive Woodward still managed to conjure up a surprise when he announced on the Tuesday in Melbourne the team to face Australia. Two changes were made to the starting fifteen, with a further three on the bench. Gloucester props Phil Vickery and Trevor Woodman would be reunited for the first time since they were chosen for the opening international of the season against New Zealand seven months previously. Graham Rowntree, who performed so well in Wellington, dropped out of the squad completely, while Jason Leonard, who could cover at both loose- and tighthead, moved to the bench.

LEFT England's pack piles on the pressure on the Wallaby line.

OVERLEAF The scene inside the enclosed Telstra Dome in Melbourne.

tree. Even though I knew what I wanted to do, win or lose against the All Blacks, I didn't tell the players until Tuesday morning. Graham's not been dropped. There are four outstanding props here and we want to see how they go. The same is true of the bench changes.'

Woodman therefore would end the international season as he had started it, in the England team, high with expectation. In between he had been struggling with injury. The twenty-six-year-old Cornishman injured his neck just a couple of days after making his starting debut against New Zealand, having previously collected five caps in three years as a substitute. The injury was not supposed to be serious, but it put him out of the game for three months.

'It was a bit of a surprise to get selected, given that the boys went so well on Saturday,' Woodman admitted. 'I've had to keep working on rehabilitation right through the season to make sure my neck is all right. It was unfortunate at the time because there was a thought that the problem might cure itself, but we decided to operate and take a disc away from the neck. It went well and I came back a month earlier than expected. I don't worry about the neck. It's the nature of the sport to get injuries.'

Jonny Wilkinson, meanwhile, was dealing with the fact that, by his own extraordinary standards, his performance against New Zealand fell a little short of the norm. Although his goal-kicking had been exemplary, and his defence predictably rock solid, his punting had been loose. 'I didn't take the full chance against the All Blacks,' he said. 'I've beaten myself up about it. You do get down about things like that, but come the middle of the following week running up to another test match the key is to put those feelings to one side and kick-start the enthusiasm. It's not been difficult to do that. None of us has ever beaten Australia here so there's a huge challenge to relish. I was happy with my preparation going into last week, so

Among the substitutes, Alex King stepped up for Paul Grayson, a fit-again Matt Dawson was preferred to Andy Gomarsall, while reserve hookers Dorian West and Mark Regan traded places.

'I'd made my mind up before the start of this trip that I wanted to swap around the front rows,' Woodward explained. 'It's an ideal opportunity to take a look at these guys. It's tough to explain to players why they're not in a test squad and that's been the case with Graham Rown-

I'm not worried on that score. It was partly the conditions that were tricky, and partly mechanical matters that I'll work on to put right.' He was also concerned about the threat from Australia. 'I think there's no doubt that it's going to be a lot harder – without the conditions, with Australia coming off a good win – than it was against New Zealand,' he argued. 'I view Australia as the world champions.'

Wilkinson had created a great deal of interest Down Under, so much so that his captain, Martin Johnson, was asked how he felt the still-young man had coped with such a burden. 'It is something he has handled pretty well,' answered Johnson. 'He has been playing at the top level for five years and I don't think it worries him. Jonny knows that there is a team there with him as well. It isn't just him. He hasn't the mindset that he has to do everything. There is a lot of experience around him.'

At least Wilkinson, who had scored an incredible sixty points in his last three test matches against Australia, would not be having to deal with a swirling wind this time. The roof of the Telstra Dome, it was announced, would be closed for the game. 'As a stand-off you can't ask for better conditions than we're going to get,' Wilkinson responded. 'You're pretty much guaranteed the ball is going to fall where you expect it to fall.' Woodward endorsed this. 'As a coach I want the roof closed,' he said. 'Whether it's right or wrong for rugby is another question. England are at their best on fast, hard surfaces. It might surprise some people down here to hear that, but that's what we want, although now that I've revealed that, pressure will probably come on to open it. To be honest, I find it very amusing that people don't understand that we want to play on a fast track.'

The following day Australia named their side, with the main talking-point being Nathan Grey, who, as predicted, would be starting at ten opposite Wilkinson. The New South Wales centre had previously played just forty minutes of test-match rugby in this position, also against England, at Twickenham three years before. Coming on as a second-half substitute, Grey and the rest of the Australian team had suffered defeat on that occasion. Apart from that, his experience was limited to a few club matches for Clive Woodward's old Sydney club at Manly, and one Super 12 outing for the Waratahs.

'This is a massive challenge for me, especially against Jonny,' said Grey. 'I don't think I can shut him down on

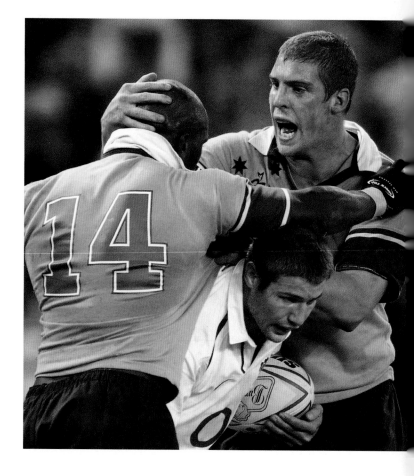

ABOVE Ben Cohen is the meat in an Australian sandwich.

RIGHT Chris Latham has to escape from Dallaglio and Thompson.

my own. It's a matter of the whole side trying to focus on shutting him down. England will know how to handle the tough situations. That's where they'll be better than the Lions.' Coach Jones clearly had high hopes for his new stand-off, in spite of his inexperience. 'Nathan's an aggressive player and the sort of players who affect Wilkinson are those who are in his face,' Jones explained. 'We're confident our team can play the kind of game to unsettle England.' Woodward, meanwhile, also recognised the likelihood of Grey's plans. 'He's a tough player and they will probably have him running straight at Wilkinson to try to take him out that way,' he predicted. 'He's a talented player, and not a lot different to Flatley.'

Ben Cohen also received praise from the Wallabies. 'Ben is big and strong and there isn't much he can't do,' said right-wing Wendell Sailor. 'I have learned a lot from him. He is a new-age winger.' Coach Jones added, 'Cohen is probably the best winger in the Northern Hemisphere.'

Will Greenwood, meanwhile, would be winning his fortieth cap in a hugely successful, if injury-ravaged, career. The fact that this would be the first time Greenwood had played a test match in Australia underlines this point. He missed the Sydney clash in 1997 due to a head injury, the visit a year later because of a shoulder operation, the Stadium Australia encounter in 1999 as a result of groin surgery and the Lions series in 2001 because of a leg problem. Now, at last, he would be playing, and such was his positive mood that he was not going to allow jibes emanating from the Australian media and the Wallaby camp to bother him. 'You try to earn respect, but if people don't respect you then that is their prerogative,' he said, with a philosophical shrug of his shoulders. 'I just hope real rugby fans think, Fair play, these England boys are doing okay. At the moment in world rugby we can look all opposing teams in the eye. That doesn't mean we will win, but we are competing and giving ourselves every chance each time.'

David Campese's predictable criticisms of England were also dismissed by the tall inside centre. 'I don't give two hoots what a bloke who won the World Cup in 1991 has to say about us,' Greenwood added. 'I am sure his sentiments are echoed by many down here, but we have shown we can win a dogfight away from home and to do it back to back would be fantastic. People say we struggle to play on a dry, fast track, but long gone are the days when Twickenham looked like a cabbage patch. They say we can't win away from home, but I should think the results in Ireland and New Zealand have gone some way to dispelling that.'

Wendell Sailor, the former Australian rugby league superstar turned union man, had something more positive to say about England, or at least about his fellow convert, Jason Robinson. 'I have followed Jason's transition closely,' he revealed. 'I spoke to him about a few things last year and I was saying how I was struggling to get the ball, and he told me I just had to find ways to get into the game.'

Robinson was clearly impressed. 'He must be doing

something right,' he said. 'He is playing in one of the best teams in the world and you don't get there if you're an average player. He still has things to work on, as we all have, and he is still new to the game. I went through all that. When you are playing at the highest level, people expect you to perform and know the game inside out from the start, but it is not quite as easy as that.'

say you're not good enough, then fair enough, but too old? That doesn't mean anything, does it? What I try to do is get there early, get hands on the ball, and quite often the player who's taken it into contact is holding on to the ball. If he'd let it go, it would be quick, because I'd pick it up and play it. It's the same as Phil Waugh and George Smith try to do with Australia.'

LEFT Jason Robinson crunches into Phil Waugh.

RIGHT Dead-eyed Jonny strikes again.

Neil Back, having been sin-binned the previous weekend against the All Blacks for killing the ball, was defending himself once again, not only for that misdemeanour but concerning his age. 'Too old?' he asked one inquisitor. 'You're either good enough or you're not. If people

His back-row colleague Lawrence Dallaglio was clearly looking forward to the test, especially as he had played only once before in an England shirt in Australia. 'That was immediately after the 1997 Lions tour, which was a bit of a crazy fixture in itself. I was kind of asleep five

ABOVE Tindall looks for support in the tackle.

minutes before kick-off, so it represents a unique challenge for us to try to do something that no England team has ever done before and win in Australia.' He wasn't going to read too much into whatever the result was going to be, however. 'People mustn't forget that the Wallabies are the current world champions, and regardless of what happens, they hold that title until the next World Cup,' he insisted. 'For me they've been the outstanding team of the last three or four years.'

On the eve of the test match both parties had a final chance to say their piece, as points were seemingly being scored off the pitch. Clive Woodward was in a bullish mood. 'I believe England can win wherever we are, whoever we are playing and in whatever conditions,' he said, injecting massive confidence into his team in the process. He added, 'We are not here to entertain: we are here to win, which is what we are paid to do. You don't get points for style. You get points for winning, and that's what we are all about. After our defeat of New Zealand last week,

this is an ideal opportunity to go for back-to-back wins against the two best teams. It's a great match-up between two world-class teams and it's good to have come here at full strength. If we're going to be successful at the World Cup in October, these are the challenges we have to meet.'

Meanwhile, over at the Wallaby camp coach Eddie Jones revealed that he had met with Irish referee David McHugh on the Thursday night to reiterate a point he had already made in previous news conferences that McHugh must officiate the contest to the letter of the law. 'We've got one of the most influential referees in the world in charge of the game,' said Jones, 'and, hopefully, he'll be very strict on enforcing the tackle and ruck laws.' Woodward, in his meeting with McHugh, had stressed that England intended to compete in the scrum, the line-

ABOVE The unfortunate Phil Waugh gets boshed again.

out and restart, but most ferociously at the breakdown, 'but within the laws'. George Gregan, the Australian captain, had his say, too: 'If he [McHugh] can interpret the match in a way that allows free-flowing rugby, then I'm sure that's what you'll see.'

As for England, Jones wanted to make a few further points. 'I don't think tries are an indicator of success in games against England,' he continued. 'It's about field position. You've got to get dominant field position. They do it so well and certainly our aim on Saturday is to dominate that area. Of course, Wilkinson is outstanding. He can kick from sixty metres out, maybe even further indoors in the Telstra Dome. But we're not going to win a kicking duel. We want to go out and play rugby.'

The former Wallaby captain John Eales summed up the mood of the whole of Australia as the country, even

the Australian Rules-dominated city of Melbourne, prepared itself for another major sporting clash between these two age-old rivals. 'One thing you can be sure of is that everyone in the world will be going for Australia against England unless they're English,' he said. 'There is one team that everyone hates to see win, and that's England.'

Number eight Toutai Kefu backed these sentiments. 'They're the last team you ever want to lose to,' said the man who had famously branded England's pack as 'Dad's Army' earlier in the year. 'Aussies love to beat the Poms at everything. But you have to play well to do that. If you allow them to get on to the front foot early, then they will overrun you. Two years ago at Twickenham we were really shocked when they started rattling through the phases. We just weren't used to them doing that. We mustn't let them get away to that sort of start.'

And so the stage was set by the Saturday evening. The Telstra Dome was just about full to capacity and, with the roof closed, was bursting with atmosphere as the watching crowd was treated to a sensational test match, if not the result that most inside desired. For England won in comprehensive style to rubber-stamp their position as the world's leading nation and, as of the end of June, with four months to go, as favourites to win the World Cup.

After ten previous attempts and forty years of failure, England finally claimed their first win on Australian soil. Outscoring Australia by three tries to one, and enjoying massive supremacy in possession and territory, England dealt the Wallabies the kind of beating which just a couple of years before would have been unthinkable. And if England had managed to convert some of the innumerable scoring chances they missed, and if they hadn't let Sailor sneak in for a late consolation try, the drubbing would have been astronomical.

First the Grand Slam, then only their second ever win in New Zealand. Now this. The vast majority of the 54,000 crowd had trudged disconsolately out of the stadium before Martin Johnson was presented with the Cook Cup to hoist high above his shoulders. We can be pretty certain that he couldn't care less about the lack of an audience, as this was surely one of his sweetest moments in the game. It was here, two years before, when the venue was named the Colonial Stadium, that his British and Irish Lions had thrown away a lead, the match and, ultimately, the series to Australia. This time, in marked contrast, English rugby enjoyed one of its greatest triumphs.

The records would keep on tumbling to the unstoppable force that was Clive Woodward's England team. This was a record-stretching thirteenth straight test win and a fourth consecutive victory over the Wallabies. Wrongly criticised for their supposedly dour win over the

LEFT AND ABOVE Ben Cohen's second-half try wraps up the game.

All Blacks the week before, England responded in style, throwing the ball around expansively in the perfect conditions created by the indoor environment. So much for boring, one-dimensional England. In the space of a week they had adapted superbly to the widely contrasting conditions thrown at them by a wet and windy Wellington and a dead-calm, bone-dry Melbourne.

Even if Australia were missing a number of key players such as George Smith, Stephen Larkham, Matt Burke and Stirling Mortlock, they had prepared themselves specifically in their three June tests to win this particular international. Using a technique suggested to them by the successful Australian swimming team, they overtrained for the matches against Ireland and Wales, which explains why they were less than impressive in these supposedly easy games, certainly against the latter. They then reduced the training workload to be in perfect physical condition for England. When they were not criticising England's style of play during the week, they were telling everyone that they had the best preparation imaginable for this test match. It would be, so they promised, their first 'peak' of the season.

Despite all of this, England bossed the proceedings. As against the All Blacks, their defence was rock solid, but this time they added some free-flowing moves from a

back line in which Will Greenwood, Mike Tindall and Ben Cohen scored masterful tries.

There was also a lot of yardage made up front by Lawrence Dallaglio, Steve Thompson, Phil Vickery, Trevor Woodman and, in particular, man-of-the-match Martin Johnson. The captain was involved on four separate occasions in a fourteen-phase move that led to a try after just seven minutes. 'I just kept on being in the right place at the right time,' said Johnson later nonchalantly. Neil Back, Kyran Bracken and Jason Robinson had all been thwarted on the line, but eventually the Wallaby defence broke to allow Greenwood the chance to bulldoze his way past Steve Kefu and David Giffin to score his twenty-fifth international try. It was close enough to the posts to make the conversion a formality for Jonny Wilkinson, and to create the perfect start for England.

'After all those phases we were going to score at some point,' insisted Greenwood. 'It would have been one hell of a shame to have come away with nothing after all that possession and territory. Mind you, I was also enjoying seeing the ball flying around so much between all the players, forwards included, so I rather spoiled the show by scoring and preventing any more phases.'

Joe Roff's 10th-minute penalty briefly cut the arrears and only Chris Latham's inability to catch Roff's sharp pass after the Wallaby wing had launched a brilliant counter-attack prevented the full-back from scoring a try.

It would prove a costly error, because England pulled further away with a second try eight minutes before the break. In a fantastic show of hand-speed and passing skills, the ball went from Johnson to Dallaglio, then on to the surging Woodman. The move faltered for a split second when he found Back, whose attempted pass was deflected by a stray Wallaby hand, but Wilkinson, Thompson and Greenwood conjured up a thrilling one-touch exchange to send Tindall over in the corner.

It was only a few months previously that Tindall's place in the starting fifteen had been questioned, but now, having gone over for the key try in the Grand Slam win in Dublin, the Bath outside centre had scored the crucial second try that eased England into a healthy lead. 'It's a toss up now to decide which of the two tries was better in the circumstances,' Tindall said. 'The Irish try played a major part in us going on to win that Slam, but to score such an important try at such an important time as we go on to win for the first time ever in Australia must get pretty close. As soon as I caught the ball and looked up to see the try line and no one in front of me I knew I was going to score.'

Then came England's only worrying period of the game. Twice before the interval Wilkinson opted to send cross-field kicks towards wing Cohen, a ploy that has proved very successful in the past. However, his first effort was a fraction too long, as Sailor bore down on Cohen, and his second too short, throwing away two promising opportunities to increase the lead. Early in the second half two Roff penalties nudged Australia to within three points of the visitors, but, unperturbed, England then upped the ante.

First Wilkinson landed a penalty. Then he teed up a spectacular try for Cohen, his twenty-first in just twenty-seven tests. Cohen had scored the winning try against Australia at Twickenham the previous November, and the Northampton wing now found the perfect angle to receive Wilkinson's short pass forty metres out. He immediately burst through the Wallaby line, and then went round a flat-footed Latham to score close to the posts. Thus ended any lingering doubts about the outcome of this game.

Just before he had emerged from the players' tunnel at the start of the game, Cohen had read a message from an old school friend. 'You're doing something we all used to dream about as lads and still do,' it read. 'You're living the dream. Go out and do us proud.' Cohen certainly did that. 'It was a lovely pass from Jonny and as I collected at speed I was away. I always held the advantage over Latham because I was running at him at pace and he was stationary, but it was still a great feeling once I knew I had the beating of him and I could see the line getting close. It was a similar try to the one I scored at Twickenham against the All Blacks, but this time I didn't need to produce a swallow dive. I knew I was going to make it to the line.'

One of the highlights of the game then followed, when the English pack drove their Wallaby counterparts from a line-out maul nearly forty metres for what looked sure to be another try. 'Surprisingly, it collapsed two metres from the Australian line,' explained Martin Johnson later. 'Very strange, that.' Note that the drive came from a line-out. Steve Thompson's throwing-in was so perfect that England claimed a 100 per cent line-out record on their own throws for the first time in three years.

There was just enough time for Sailor to drop another hint that he is going to be a major threat in the World Cup when, in injury-time, he beat six English players with a meandering run from forty metres out to score arguably the best try of the night. He did touch down in the corner, though, and Roff was unable to convert. It was a crucial miss because it meant Australia were still eight points, and two scores, behind England with just a few seconds remaining.

However, there was still time for two final acts from the England backs to rub yet more salt into the Wallaby wound. First Josh Lewsey flattened Mat Rogers with a perfectly legal but deadly hit that proved to be the tackle of the night. 'I was quite pleased with that one,' a smiling Lewsey said later. 'Good hit, wasn't it?' said an approving Tindall, who was nearest to the carnage. It took Rogers the best part of three minutes to raise himself from the turf. Then Wilkinson slotted home a penalty with literally just a couple of seconds remaining to make the margin of victory a very comfortable eleven points.

Afterwards Clive Woodward paid tribute to all his men, but singled out his captain for a special mention. 'It was a big, big win and I can't praise my players enough, especially Martin,' said Woodward. 'He's been a brilliant leader on the pitch and off it as well, where he played an instrumental part in our strongest team making the trip to New Zealand and Australia. He has ensured that our attitude on this tour has been first class, and his own performance today was exceptional. He has gone from strength to strength and has fronted up now to both the All Blacks and the Wallabies.'

To his Australian counterpart Eddie Jones, Woodward was not so willing to dish out the plaudits. 'The team didn't need motivation from me,' insisted the England Head Coach. 'Eddie Jones did the job. You get labelled by the opposition coach but you just have to get on with winning. I don't believe in pressurising the referee. It was premeditated and it was not good for the sport. I'm just pleased that we've made it four wins out of four against Jones. We'll wait until the World Cup in October in Australia and the next anti-English media campaign orchestrated by him. We'll thrive on it. We'll happily enter the

RIGHT Martin Johnson soars high to claim the ball.

World Cup as favourites. And we'll be comfortable with that tag.'

Lawrence Dallaglio was also less than impressed by the pre-match antics of the Australian coach. 'It motivated us a bit more, to show people that they don't fully appreciate how the game in the Northern Hemisphere has developed,' he said. 'We've taken a lot of stick over here and we've answered it in the best way possible. If you're good enough, age is irrelevant. Some players continue to reach outstanding levels of fitness. The older they get, the better they are.'

Jason Robinson was simply delighted, not just with this sensational tour Down Under, but with life in general. After all, this was a man who had taken a big gamble when leaving rugby league for union three years previously. 'We've proved beyond doubt that this England team can beat anyone, anywhere and at any time,' he said. 'Everything now seems to be in place for us to achieve the ultimate and win the World Cup. Losing is no longer an option. We will be going for the main prize. There's been a belief in the squad for some time that we are capable of

ABOVE A victorious England squad face the world's press photographers.

something exceptional. That belief grows stronger with each game and now we have answered those people who didn't believe we could win away from Twickenham. Beating Australia is special, but, then again, we're a special team. That's what Clive Woodward spelled out to me when we first talked about switching codes. I reckon I'm on the verge now of playing a big part in it all.'

The morning after there was a mixture of satisfaction and forward planning in the England camp. Woodward was still on an understandable high. 'The greater the pressure, the better our guys perform,' he said. 'We have no fear now about playing anyone, anywhere. We relish the pressure on us. It's been a perfect trip for us. We've had no injuries and got good results. It sets us up for the World Cup. Four years ago we went into that tournament with our fingers crossed. This time we will have prepared properly and all we can do as coaches is to give Martin Johnson and his team every chance of doing something special in their lives. Our whole mindset now switches to the World Cup.'

It really was the perfect way to round off a perfect season. A hat-trick of wins over the Southern Hemisphere giants at Twickenham, a first Grand Slam in eight years, two historic wins in New Zealand, and then the first defeat of Australia in Australia. Not even Woodward and Johnson would have dreamed of such a season.

The Melbourne victory made it ten successive wins over the big three from the Southern Hemisphere, too, England's last defeat coming in Pretoria back in 2000. Moreover, this was England's first invincible season since 1956–7, when England played only four times. The only side to get even close to this current crop of players was Temple Gurdon's team of 1882–7, his squad winning ten and drawing two.

On their way home, the English players took a three-day detour to Perth. There they inspected the Subiaco Oval, where they would be playing their World Cup group games, and scouted the team hotel and other facilities. For the team a holiday then beckoned, and the chance to spend some precious time with their loved ones.

The vacation would be short, though. Training camps, squad announcements, selections and three warm-up internationals would all be looming as the summer turned to autumn. None of England's incredible achievements of the heady past eight months would guarantee that the team would go on to win the World Cup, of course. But they would be entering the tournament with a very strong case indeed.

Besides, never mind the World Cup: the ten out of ten, and all the milestones recorded in the process, was a huge achievement in its own right. As Martin Johnson put it, in his characteristic, understated style, 'It's not too bad a job done, is it?' Indeed it was not. Not too bad at all.

BELOW Clive Woodward and assistant coach Andy Robinson savour the moment.

WORLD CUP DETAILS

(All times UK)

Pool A	Australia, Argentina, Ireland, Romania, Namibia
Pool B	France, Scotland, Fiji, Japan
Pool C	England, South Africa, Manu Samoa, Uruguay, Georgia
Pool D	New Zealand, Wales, Canada, Italy

Fri, Oct 10	Australia v Argentina (A)	11 am, Sydney
Sat, Oct 11	New Zealand v Italy (D)	5.30 am, Melbourne
Sat, Oct 11	France v Fiji (B)	8 am, Brisbane
Sat, Oct 11	Ireland v Romania (A)	10.30 am, Gosford
Sat, Oct 11	South Africa v Uruguay (C)	1 pm, Perth
Sun, Oct 12	Wales v Canada (D)	9 am, Melbourne
Sun, Oct 12	**ENGLAND** v Georgia (C)	1 pm, Perth
Tue, Oct 14	Argentina v Namibia (A)	10.30 am, Gosford
Wed, Oct 15	Fiji v USA (B)	8 am, Brisbane
Wed, Oct 15	Italy v Tonga (D)	10.30 am, Canberra
Wed, Oct 15	Manu Samoa v Uruguay (C)	1 pm, Perth
Fri, Oct 17	New Zealand v Canada (D)	10.30 am, Melbourne
Sat, Oct 18	Australia v Romania (A)	7.30 am, Brisbane
Sat, Oct 18	France v Japan (B)	10 am, Townsville
Sat, Oct 18	**ENGLAND** v South Africa (C)	1 pm, Perth
Sun, Oct 19	Wales v USA (B)	9 am, Canberra
Sun, Oct 19	Ireland v Namibia (A)	10.30 am, Sydney
Sun, Oct 19	Georgia v Manu Samoa (C)	1 pm, Perth
Mon, Oct 20	Scotland v USA (B)	10.30 am, Brisbane
Tue, Oct 21	Italy v Canada (D)	10.30 am, Canberra
Wed, Oct 22	Argentina v Romania (A)	11 am, Sydney
Thu, Oct 23	Fiji v Japan (B)	11 am, Townsville
Fri, Oct 24	New Zealand v Tonga (D)	8.30 am, Brisbane
Fri, Oct 24	South Africa v Georgia (C)	11 am, Sydney
Sat, Oct 25	Australia v Namibia (A)	6 am, Adelaide
Sat, Oct 25	Italy v Wales (D)	9 am, Canberra
Sat, Oct 25	France v Scotland (B)	11 am, Sydney
Sun, Oct 26	**ENGLAND** v Manu Samoa (C)	7 am, Melbourne
Sun, Oct 26	Argentina v Ireland (A)	9.30 am, Adelaide
Mon, Oct 27	Japan v USA (B)	8.30 am, Gosford
Tue, Oct 28	Georgia v Uruguay (C)	8.30 am, Sydney
Wed, Oct 29	Canada v Tonga (D)	8.30 am, Wollongong
Thu, Oct 30	Romania v Namibia (A)	11 am, Launceston
Fri, Oct 31	France v USA (B)	8.30 am, Wollongong
Sat, Nov 1	Scotland v Fiji (B)	4 am, Sydney
Sat, Nov 1	South Africa v Manu Samoa (C)	7 am, Brisbane
Sat, Nov 1	Australia v Ireland (A)	9.30 am, Melbourne
Sun, Nov 2	**ENGLAND** v Uruguay (C)	7 am, Brisbane
Sun, Nov 2	New Zealand v Wales (D)	9.30 am, Sydney

Quarter-Finals

Sat, Nov 8	Winner D v Runner-up C	7.30 am, Melbourne
Sat, Nov 8	Winner A v Runner-up B	10 am, Brisbane
Sun, Nov 9	Winner B v Runner-up A	7.30 am, Melbourne
Sun, Nov 9	Winner C v Runner-up D	10 am, Brisbane

Semi-Finals

| Sat, Nov 15 | Winner QF1 v Winner QF 2 | 9 am, Sydney |
| Sun, Nov 16 | Winner QF3 v Winner QF4 | 9 am, Sydney |

Third Place Play-Off

| Thu, Nov 20 | 9 am, Sydney |

WORLD CUP FINAL

| Sat, Nov 22 | 9 am, Sydney |

WORLD CUP

1987   NEW ZEALAND

Winners: New Zealand. Runners-up: France

1991   ENGLAND, INCORPORATING FRANCE, WALES, SCOTLAND AND IRELAND

Winners: Australia. Runners-up: England

1995   SOUTH AFRICA

Winners: South Africa. Runners-up: New Zealand

1999   Wales, incorporating British Isles & France

Winners: Australia. Runners-up: France

ENGLAND'S WORLD CUP RECORD

1987:	Quarter-finals: Lost to Wales
1991:	Finalists: Lost to Australia
1995:	Semi-finalists: Lost to New Zealand
1999:	Quarter-finalists: Lost to South Africa

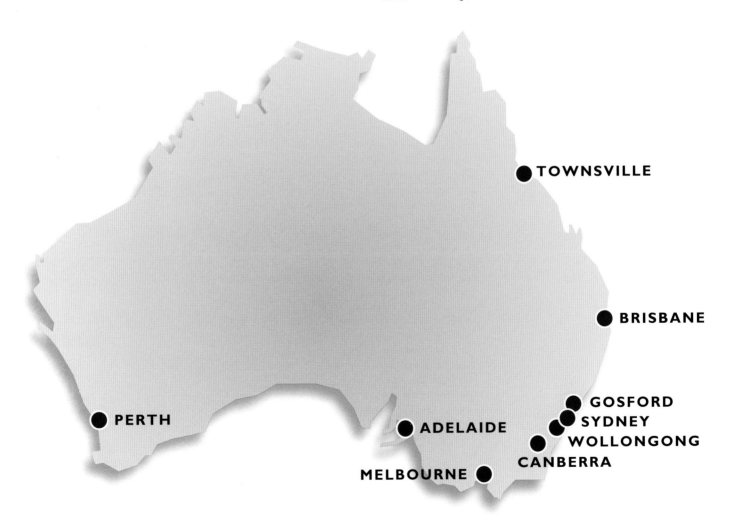

PICTURE CREDITS

Photographs supplied by Gettyimages

page 1   David Rogers
page 12   David Rogers (above)
page 13   David Rogers (above)
page 14   Jamie McDonald (right)
page 15   David Rogers
page 16   David Rogers (above)
page 17   Ben Radford (below)
page 18   Ben Radford
page 19   John Gichigi
page 20   Jamie McDonald (left)
page 21   Jamie McDonald (right)
page 22   Ben Radford
page 23   Ben Radford
page 25   David Rogers
page 28   David Rogers
page 29   Mike Hewitt
page 31   David Rogers
page 32   Mark Thompson (left)
page 32-3   David Rogers (right)
page 34   Mark Thompson
page 35   Mike Hewitt
page 36   David Rogers
page 37   Mike Hewitt (left)
page 37   David Rogers (right)
page 40   David Rogers
page 41   Stephen Munday
page 42   David Rogers
page 43   Stephen Munday
page 44   Stephen Munday (left)
page 44-5   Stephen Munday (right)
page 46   David Rogers
page 48   Shaun Botterill (above left)
page 48   Shaun Botterill (right)
page 49   Stephen Munday (above right)
page 50   David Rogers
page 51   David Rogers
page 52-3   David Rogers
page 53   David Rogers (above right)
page 53   David Rogers (below)
page 56   John Gichigi
page 57   Mark Thompson
page 58   Mark Thompson
page 59   Mark Thompson
page 60   Ben Radford
page 62   Jamie McDonald
page 63   Jamie McDonald
page 64   David Rogers
page 66   Jamie McDonald (above left)
page 66-7   Mark Thompson (below right)
page 67   David Rogers (above left)
page 70   David Rogers
page 71   David Rogers
page 72-3   Phil Cole (above)
page 73   Phil Cole (below)
page 74   David Rogers
page 75   Phil Cole (above)
page 75   Phil Cole (below)
page 76   Phil Cole
page 77   Phil Cole
page 79   Phil Cole

page 82   Warren Little
page 84   David Rogers
page 85   Harry How
page 86   Harry How (above left)
page 86   Harry How (below right)
page 87   Harry How (above)
page 87   David Rogers (below right)
page 88   Phil Cole
page 89   David Rogers
page 90   David Rogers
page 91   David Rogers
page 92   Phil Cole
page 93   Phil Cole (above)
page 93   Harry How (below)
page 96   David Rogers (left)
page 96-7   David Rogers (right)
page 98   Jamie McDonald
page 99   David Cannon (right)
page 100   David Rogers
page 101   Jamie McDonald
page 102   Jamie McDonald
page 103   David Rogers (right)
page 104   David Cannon (left)
page 105   David Rogers (right above)
page 105   Somebody Someone (below)
page 106   David Cannon
page 107   David Rogers
page 110   David Rogers
page 111   David Rogers
page 112   Phil Cole
page 113   David Rogers
page 114   David Rogers
page 115   Phil Cole
page 116   David Rogers
page 117   David Rogers
page 119   Christopher Lee
page 120   David Rogers
page 121   David Rogers (above & below)
page 124   David Rogers
page 126   David Rogers
page 128   David Rogers
page 129   David Rogers
page 131   David Rogers
page 132   David Rogers
page 133   David Rogers
page 134-5 David Rogers
page 136   David Rogers
page 137   David Rogers
page 140   David Rogers
page 141   David Rogers
page 142-3 Mark Dadswell
page 144-5 Mark Dadswell
page 146   Ryan Pierse
page 147   Nick Laham
page 148   Stuart Hannagan
page 149   Mark Dadswell
page 150   Nick Laham
page 151   Ryan Pierse
page 152   Robert Cianflone
page 153   Robert Cianflone
page 155   Sean Garnswort
page 156   Nick Laham

page 157   David Rogers

Team England Rugby would like to thank Ian
Stafford, Richard Prescott at the RFU, Robert Kirby
at PFD, Freddie Nuttall, Annabel Taylor and Sarah
Bentley at CSS-Stellar, Malcolm Edwards, Ian
Preece and Richard Hussey at Orion, Philip Parr,
Harry Green, Ros Ellis and Gettyimages.